A Grandparents' Guide from Land's End to John o' Groats

A Grandparents' Guide from Land's End to John o' Groats

Or 'I knew someone who did it on a bicycle'

Eileen & Herbert Witherington

WANDE Publications

First published in 1993 by
WANDE Publications
38 North Guards, Whitburn, Sunderland SR6 7AD

Cover design by Deborah Purvis

ISBN 0–9522488–0–8

Typeset in Palatino by
Wearset, Boldon, Tyne and Wear
and printed in Great Britain by
Athenaeum Press Ltd, Newcastle upon Tyne

This book is dedicated to
JOSS ACKLAND
without whose inspiration this crazy idea
would never have occurred to us.

'He gives power to the faint and to him who
has no might He increases strength.
Even the youths shall faint and be weary,
and the young men shall utterly fall.
But they who wait upon the Lord shall renew
their strength;
They shall mount up with wings as eagles.
They shall run and not be weary.
They shall walk and not faint.'

Isaiah. Ch. 40 vv 29–31.

Acknowledgements

Our list of acknowledgements is so long that it can only be briefly told.

Firstly, our thanks to those who made this book possible; to Shelagh McClure who managed to make order out of the original chaos of the diary; and to David Staward of 'Wearset', our typesetter and a fellow member of Whitburn Methodist Church, whose expert advice and encouragement were essential to the project.

Secondly, to those who helped us along the way; their names appear and reappear in the pages of this book.

Thirdly, to that massive band of warm-hearted folk who sponsored us cheerfully, willingly and recklessly for the cause of Christian Aid. The TV interviewer who talked to us on the Cotswold Way asked if we had found that people were saturated with demands for giving. Our answer was very emphatic – 'Not in our experience'. Their names – or most of them – were recorded in the Christian Aid sponsorship forms, which we no longer have, but we say a very big 'thank you' to them all. The total amount contributed at the time of the walk was just over £6,500, which we hope will be increased by the sale of this book. (If you are reading this and are wondering whether to buy it, that's just the excuse you needed.)

Contents

Elderly
people

Introduction

'I know someone who did it on a bicycle.' Whenever you are walking with packs on your back, especially in odd places such as outside the Pump Room at Bath or through the centre of Glasgow, it is to be expected that folk will stop and ask you where you have come from and where you are going. And we told them, not at all in that insufferable 'haven't-we-done-well' manner but rather in an effort to convince ourselves that this was what we had set out to do. We soon discovered when Land's End and John o' Groats were mentioned in one breath invariably there was the same response. They knew someone who had done it on a bicycle. That doesn't surprise us in any way. The further north we toiled up Scotland, the more bicycles that passed us, displaying large hoardings that informed everyone that it was on behalf of this or that good cause, sometimes accompanied by large vans or mobile houses, all riders in deadly earnest and obviously intent on reaching the other end within the fortnight allocated from their holidays for this particular journey. As we waited at John o' Groats for the car that was to take us to Thurso station – and it was only a minute or two late – two perspiring cyclists arrived in that triumphant state of exhaustion which could only signify that they had come from 'the other end'. It is a major factor in the economic prosperity of Caithness – a growth industry without any doubt, with records constantly being broken for travelling the greatest distance between two points in the British Isles by an extraordinary variety of transport. So it is no wonder that everyone knows someone who has done it on a bicycle. It is the obvious alternative title for this book.

Our story begins in the early days of 1990 when we watched, along with the usual millions of viewers, Joss Ackland in a highly imaginative epic entitled *The First and the Last*. A recently retired gentleman set out from Land's End to fulfil an ambition to walk to the other end. Through a long series of intriguing adventures and mishaps and physical problems, after four hours of the most exhausting viewing, he reached his goal – his Heavenly City, or its Scottish equivalent. 'Why don't we do that?' we said to each other, and to make sure that we were being serious we wrote a date in our diaries, not this year (we had too much to do this year), but next, as soon as the weather might be expected to be reasonable – say the middle of April, Monday, the 15th, South to North, so that the sun (what funny ideas some people have!) would not be constantly in our eyes, and we would be going to the cooler north as the summer progressed. Like the majority of planners we got it all wrong.

The title of this book is 'A grandparents' guide from Land's End to John o' Groats'. The very first lesson to be learnt is when you make a decision like this one you don't think about it. Once you start thinking it's a dead duck. 'Thus conscience (that means 'thinking') does make cowards of us all', says Hamlet. Think about blisters and days in the rain and the sheer labour of walking for months on end and you let out the coward in you who says, 'What me? Not likely!' Anyway, there are plenty of well-meaning friends who will do that sort of thinking for you, who will ask you how you get cash or pay the Access bills, where do you stay in that bleak god-forsaken spot in the wilderness of central Sutherland, do you know that your spine begins to crumble and that the pain of corns only gets worse not better? If anyone asks you these sorts of questions, remember it is the voice of the Devil. Don't listen to him, either to that little voice inside you that constantly asks, 'Do you really know what you are doing?' or to your well-meaning neighbour

First and Last

who insists on reminding you that you aren't as young as you used to be. Who is for that matter?

We have one advantage over Joss Ackland; he had never walked more than three miles. Some years ago, after our children had left home and we were free (which is what they thought they were) we realised we were in a rut. We were in a Lakeland rut – we never got further than Wastwater or higher than Scafell. Ruts are fatal: you end up getting buried in them. So when Herbert said, 'We are in a rut', there and then Eileen climbed out of it. 'Let's go to the Himalayas,' she said. We did, and there we learned some of the great secrets of long distance walking; such as, it is all a question of putting one foot in front of the other; such as (and you learn this in church, but in long distance walking you apply it), take no anxious thought for the morrow, each day has troubles enough of its own; or the great lesson of the Himalayan trek from our dear friend Betty, when after the first three or four days of unimagined and demoralising hardship she volunteered the opinion that 'one day you will discover that you are enjoying it'. And we did discover it. It is always a shock when for the first time you encounter the experience of every morning, *every* morning, having to gird up your loins and face another day of footslogging. But before long it becomes a way of life. You smile condescendingly at those hysterical motorists tearing along the motorways on their way to hell. You recall with a sense of pity those stuck at home because they dare not take the risk. You carry all your belongings on your back. You snap your fingers at those tyrants that dominate everyday life, such as telephones, diaries, self-imposed routines. And off you go into a world of freedom which you share with the flowers and the trees, the birds and the butterflies, the skies and the sun and the wind and the rain, yes quite often the wind and the rain. Every night you stop to discover a new experience and meet new people: you greet these experiences and these people timidly, not knowing what you have let yourself in for, and you say goodbye to them the next morning with the greatest reluctance, feeling that you are parting from your dearest friend. No, it isn't always like that, but it is so frequent an experience that you come to expect it. It is part and parcel of long distance walking. Land's End to John o' Groats is a challenge, without any doubt. 'A man's reach should exceed his grasp or what's a heaven for.' That's what Browning said. Long distances are a test of will power as much as they are of physical fitness. But as far as we were concerned it was also a great exercise in escapism which was like realising a fairy tale, and whilst the waiting days passed with increasing apprehension, so did our eagerness and impatience to get going increase as well.

There are the practical details that have to be sorted out. The first practical detail that occurred to us was the simple question, 'How do you get from Land's End to John o' Groats?' Which way do you go? Later on in the diary we meet a man on the Pennine Way who is without map or compass and has never heard of Wainwright. 'How do you find your way?' we asked him. 'I go north' was the reply. Well, go north from Land's End and you should end up somewhere overlooking the Pentland Firth – after all John o' Groats is only a mile or so east of Land's End. But that was not good enough for us. We did debate a great deal the question of walking by faith; how much did we have to plan, and how much did we rely on pot-luck, or miracles as we came to regard the wonderful happenings? We never came to a final conclusion in that debate, but we both felt that we needed a route. So we wrote to the secretary of the Long Distance Walkers' Association and asked him if he could put us in touch with someone who had been that way before. He did, and Ann Sayer wrote to us by return of post giving meticulous details of the route she walked in 1980. Unfortunately it was more or less useless, because what Ann Sayer had done in 1980 was to break the women's record for walking from Land's End to John o' Groats in the ridiculous time of 13 days, 17 hours, 42 minutes, averaging 60 miles a day – a record which still stands. But she recognised that we were in a different league and handed us on to another walker from the West Country known by the name of Mac. Mac typifies that great fellowship of the road to which all long distance walkers automatically, perhaps unwittingly, belong, a fellowship of men and women who are ever ready to help each other in any and every possible way. Mac wrote us reams and reams of details of routes (all of which he had to transcribe from back to front because he had walked north to south), places to stay, problems we were likely to face and difficulties that could be overcome. He gave us the confidence and encouragement which we so badly needed and also friendship which continued throughout the months of preparation and the hundreds of miles of walking. We tried to arrange a meeting on the way, but we were several days behind schedule at the vital time and we are still only correspondents.

We had searched bookshops and mountaineering shops, as well as advertisements in numerous publications to do with walking, for some simple straightforward manual on the walk from Land's End to John o' Groats, but without any success. We did read John Hillaby and Hamish Brown, but neither managed to provide the grandparents' guide we were looking for. So for the would-be walker who is reading this with some impatience wondering when he is going to reach the 'how?' of it all, here is the tortuous plan which eventually materialised after many months of brooding and debating. You acquire a copy of the 'Long Distance Walkers' Handbook' (which is available in bookshops) and look at the maps of England and Scotland with their little black lines wriggling all over the country. These black lines are our Long Distance Footpaths, dozens and dozens of them in England, very few – alas! – in Scotland. From these you plan your overall strategy. The Handbook provides you with details of OS maps covering each and every walk, and where publications describing the walk and particulars of accommodation can be obtained. And Bob's your Uncle. We ended up with 34 OS maps and 8 publications on individual walks, in addition to a Route Planning Map of Britain which was essential. Our strategy was based on the preference for walking on footpaths rather than roads. This adds many miles on to the distance of 874 miles shown by the signpost at Land's End; it also adds to the ups and downs, the roughness and the wetness underfoot, and the practical problems of finding eats and drinks and beds. Road walking, for all its confusion of noise and petrol fumes, is very much quicker; often when we began to wonder if we would ever reach the other end at the snail's pace we were achieving on the footpaths, we would sneak off on to some convenient stretch of road for a few miles and immediately increase our rate of progress. The overall plan unfolds throughout the pages of the diary, but here are the details which we prepared for the many loving folk who were concerned about our whereabouts for three months – and a few comments added in retrospect which may, or may not, be helpful:

1 Land's End to Barnstable. By North Cornwall Coastal Footpath and road. There was rather more road than originally intended. The footpath, breathtakingly spectacular on most of its way, was extremely hard going and the road, which was never far away, was a constant temptation. But never for very long; the lure of the path repeatedly drew us back to the cliffs.
2 Barnstable to Taunton. By road, via South Molton, Bampton, Wiviliscombe. It took a long time to reach the end of Cornwall and even in the planning stage we realised the necessity of getting a move on. So we cut across the centre of Devon and into Somerset.
3 Taunton to Bath. By the Somerset Way. The publication

had originally horrified us with the time-wasting meanderings of the route. In fact it turned out as we feared and we reverted to the road. To be fair to the writer, he was suggesting a route which took in the places and sites of historical interest, but we really did not have the time or energy to be interested in history.

4 Bath to Chipping Campden. By the Cotswold Way. Another very undulating and tough route, as well as being circuitous – its total of 102 miles covers a distance of 50 miles as the crow flies. But we did more or less stick to it. Very well signposted.

5 Chipping Campden to Mitford. By the Heart of England Way. Recently opened, and again well signposted. It very cleverly avoids the massive industrial centres like Birmingham and Coventry. We did deviate to go into Stratford as we wanted to visit the theatre. Just our luck! When we arrived there was nothing on for the next three days.

6 Mitford to Congleton. By the Staffordshire Way, or part of it. On the final day when it was raining cats and dogs, we chickened out of the appointed way which led up into the clouds, and followed the A53 from Leek to Buxton. That was bad enough.

7 Congleton to Edale. By the Cestrian Link Way – a footpath which connects Offa's Dyke in North Wales with the Pennine Way. We were concerned only with the last few miles of it.

8 Edale to Settle. By the Pennine Way. Yes, we tried to avoid it. All Wainwright's horrendous descriptions of the Pennine Way (quote – 'cheer up, there's worse to come') have been abundantly confirmed by our own experience, and it didn't help to read a letter from a friend who warned us off it, describing how he had recently submerged up to his armpits on Cheviot. We did as little as we could get away with. In our short spell we had to do two consecutive days on road (a much longer distance) because we were convinced that if we had continued on the Way we would never have been heard of again. It lived up to its reputation and we were thankful to come off at Airton and make for Settle along the road. Over the

following few days we would gaze in horror at the cloud covering all signs of Cross Fell and its neighbours and think of those poor devils we had met who were still in hell. Thankfully, we weren't.

9 Settle to Carlisle. By the Settle to Carlisle Walk – another newly contrived walk which had the great advantages of following the railway and avoiding the Pennine Way. By this time the weather had really settled down to do its worst, and again we were forced onto roads for self-preservation.

10 Carlisle to Glasgow. The great question mark. Mac followed the Burns Heritage Trail which was a very attractive route but on our reckoning added 5 days to the marathon. We kept our options open, but had a hunch that by the time we reached it we would be prepared to endure the A74 for the best part of a week. We were. The walker is also faced with 25 miles of Glasgow, its suburbs and surrounds – a necessary discipline, Mac called it. It was certainly discipline.

11 Glasgow (Milngavie) to Fort William. By the West Highland Way. One of the very few long distance footpaths in Scotland. We had done it ten years previously, soon after it was opened. A walk of great character and bad weather, we recalled. It still is.

12 Fort William to Inverness. Some years ago we had read of the prospect of a long distance footpath taking the walker up the Caledonian Canal and the Great Glen. We wrote to the authorities to enquire if it was open by now. They replied, very kindly and graciously, to say that it was still a prospect. They suggested forestry roads and General Wade's road, which we followed, but there was a lot of traffic on the other parts.

13 Inverness to John o' Groats. Mac had gone north from Bonar Bridge to Bettyhill and along the top (he had done it the other way round of course, but he always managed to write as if he was going in the same direction as we were). Late into the night we had pondered on the wide open spaces on the OS maps. One of our problems in planning is that we are very definitely not 20 mile-a-

dayers: we are comfortable at 10, or 12 on a good day, perhaps even 15 in sheer necessity. But we planned the whole route on the basis of 10–12 miles per day, and it did seem that here we might be lost in the wilderness, unable to walk any further. Being a prudent man, Herbert bought the maps covering the A9 up the coast as well as Mac's route. We used the A9!

The route was painstakingly traced and marked on each of the 34 OS maps. It was measured with one of those gadgets like a fountain pen, but with a little wheel instead of a nib. You add 10% to the measured distance to be on the safe side and it came out at 1100 miles. A provisional list of nightly stopping places was drawn up which totalled 89 days. It turned out to be 93. And now it was just a question of finding the route on the ground.

When are we going to begin? Patience, dear reader. For everyone who is turning over the pages of this book in idle curiosity, there is another filled with a burning desire to follow in Joss Ackland's footsteps but still with a long list of questions waiting to be answered. Where did we sleep? Wherever we could find a bed, and we never failed to do that: we never slept beneath the hedges which was Eileen's romantic idea of the wandering life. We had previously read

The Planner

in *The Guardian* of a man who walked from Cape Wrath to Land's End, and booked up accommodation for 80 nights before he started. In the first week in Scotland the sole of one of his boots dropped off, but in spite of this calamity, and the additional painful experience of shedding three toenails en route, he somehow managed to keep to his schedule. The idea of losing a day early on and having to alter, say, seventy or so reservations made our hair stand on end, so we settled for booking up as we went along. That of course had its anxieties, but they proved groundless. Herbert, who was responsible for finding the accommodation as well as the way, worried unnecessarily for 3½ months: only when Mrs Harrold said yes, she had a room, on the penultimate evening did he sleep in peace (the final night was already booked). So learn from his experience and go off in faith that the remarkable British system of B & Bs will provide for you. We took with us long lists of names and addresses gathered from the 'Ramblers' (a very useful reference book to have with you – the Ramblers Association Handbook), the AA, 'Off the Beaten Track', Mac's list of accommodation and so on, and we used them only occasionally.

The weeks we walked through England were very quiet and frequently we were the only ones staying at a particular hostelry or homestead. By the time we reached Scotland the holidays had begun so we booked up ahead for the West Highland Way where accommodation is always in demand. Otherwise we relied on the services of the Tourist Information Offices, which were usually most efficient and helpful – only in the very popular centres did they show signs of being harrassed. Not all accommodation is registered with them of course, and at times we relied on the local post office, the local inhabitants, the local Christian Aid organisers, or just that magical sign with the legend 'B & B' inscribed on it, which, as we have said, never failed to appear.

Equipment? Only two items really matter – boots and rainwear. With these you are very much dependent upon the advice received from behind the counter which, you always suspect, is influenced by salesmanship. We live at a time when the customer is no longer always right, but rather the reverse. Boots, for instance. 'Will they last a thousand miles?', we asked. We were assured that they would, and they didn't. When we mentioned the fact later on, the response was, 'But you were walking on roads.' Another pair let in water on the very first occasion they were worn in wet weather. As we hadn't started the walk, we took them back to the shop in Keswick where we had bought them. 'Where have you been walking?', we were asked. We explained. 'But', was the indignant reply, 'that's the wettest place in the Lake District'. We did mention the prospect of the Pennine Way and the West Highland that faced us, but they didn't seem too impressed. The sequel to that story was that the boots were returned to the manufacturers where they were mislaid, and eventually replaced with new. From these harrowing and uncertain beginnings our boots were an unqualified success in every one of the two and a half million steps (approximately) we each trod. We are thankful beyond words that a friend recommended the name of Chris Brasher, and we hope that we prove friends to others for passing that name on. The greatest proof of their excellence is that we did not suffer one single blister between us on the whole of the journey. They were a joy to put on in the morning and seemed to impart an additional spring into each step we took. Considering the weather we encountered from June onwards our feet kept remarkably dry, and when we did have to replace them round about halfway we bought identical fittings and were able to continue in the new boots without any discomfort. What more can we say? Your boots are your best friends.

Rainwear – the story does not have the same happy ending. We had efficient rainwear but it was heavy and bulky, and we wanted something that was light and which folded up into next to nothing. We went to look at some. 'Is it Gore-tex?', we asked. No, but the fabric absorbed so many litres of moisture per so many square metres of surface every 24 hours; we were told the exact figures at least three times but still cannot remember them. We were also assured that they were guaranteed '100% waterproof'. This story unfolds in the early pages of the diary. We returned them to the manufacturers who, without too much argument, refunded our money.

When we trekked in the Himalayas we were of course spoilt in that we had someone else to carry our belongings. The porters there are the transport system essential to every expedition for the simple reason that the tourists are incapable of carrying everything they need at high altitudes. When we returned to earth and decided to attempt Wainwright's Coast to Coast walk across the north of England, the question arose, who was going to carry our belongings? After many imaginative suggestions and a whole series of requests to friends with motor cars, we reluctantly came to the conclusion that we had to do it ourselves. It was then that we devised a scheme which has enabled us to be independent on every walk we have attempted. How? – by settling on the weight we are each going to carry and weighing every individual object before it is accepted in the final list. Have you exceeded your total weight? Throw away your pyjama tops, and carry only the lightest comb and toothbrush. Eileen bought two shirts that weighed 6 ounces each; they were left behind. We went to buy a new camera. 'What sort?' we were asked. 'The lightest.' By ruthlessly applying this system we managed to carry our raingear, spare socks, a complete set of clothes for the evening – very smart they were too – all the usual junk in a lady's sponge bag, maps, plasters, water bottle etc. etc. etc. It is quite an art packing and unpacking, but you get very proficient after three months. We came across hikers who seemed determined to include even the proverbial kitchen sink – there was one young man on his first long distance walk whose rucksack we literally could not not lift from the ground – whilst we can provide all we need in a total weight of 10–12 lbs for him and 8–10 lbs for her.

The time and distances on this particular walk of course meant that the logistics had to be much more elaborate, as we would need clean clothes – that is if anyone was ever going to let us into their homes after the first few weeks – and a regular and consecutive supply from that enormous cardboard box of OS maps. For this we enlisted the aid of our daughter, Jane, as co-ordinator-in-chief, and either she parcelled up and sent off our requirements once a fortnight to a prearranged address, or persuaded her brother or sister to do so. TV viewers will recall that this system was used by Joss Ackland thanks to his long-suffering wife.

So that is all we can pass on to the fearful would-be Land's End to John o' Groats walker in the hope that he or she will take fresh courage from our experience. Don't worry about training: the walk is the training. All it needs now is that step of faith. Can you walk 10 miles in one day? Then probably you can walk 20 in two days. And if you can walk 20 in two, then you can walk 50 in five and 100 in ten. And if you can't, take a rest and try again; and if you still can't, at least you have tried.

Two things happened before our departure. After months of preparation, one evening we came almost simultaneously to the conclusion that all this work and organisation and effort deserved some higher purpose than merely that exercise in escapism we were planning. The answer came in the post the very next morning with an appeal from Christian Aid for the African famine victims. They were being forgotten as a result of the Gulf War but desperately needed help, we read. We recognised that it would change the whole character of the walk; there would be no question of sneaking off home when we'd had enough; we had to be serious about it. But it was the Message with the capital M, one you cannot ignore; so we rang the local Christian Aid organiser, Peter Schofield, and offered our services, which were accepted. One immediate result was that we were allocated a Press Officer, Mrs Jean Taylor from Jarrow. Jean worked almost as hard as we did to raise the money and it was her incessant activity that ensured that our pictures appeared in every local newspaper and that no-one was left in any doubt about how old we were (68 and 67, by the way). Another result, not immediate but obvious in retrospect, was the probability that we would never have finished the walk if we had being doing it only for ourselves. Not only did the cause of Christian Aid give us the shove when we were tired or despondent, but we knew from the very beginning that we were surrounded by 'the great host of witnesses' as the Scriptures promise, men and women and children who were cheering us on and willing us to finish. Yes, it was a great physical exercise, entirely – so it seemed – occupied with walking, eating and sleeping. But there was something else as well, something pretty well indefinable, but a source of strength and encouragement that kept us going when our physical resources came to an end.

The other incident was very dramatic. We had watched Joss Ackland suffer from one calamity after another. We saw him soaking off his bloody socks in the bath; he lost his Access card; he 'dropped in' on his daughter in Manchester, and promptly collapsed: and yet again he collapsed in the mud of that farmyard in the Pennines and he ended up in hospital with the doctor issuing the most dire warnings. That was the drama, of course. It was what made you watch his saga for four hours on end. It didn't give us sleepless nights. But fact can be as strange as fiction. We were due to catch the train to Penzance on Monday, 15th April. The problems of going away for 3 months were becoming more and more overwhelming the nearer D-day approached, and the list of 'things to be done' grew more and more extensive until we began to wonder if we would ever reach the end. On the Saturday afternoon, Herbert came into the room where Eileen was checking her belongings for the umpteenth time. He opened his mouth to speak but no words issued forth: eventually he managed to convey to her that the symptoms of his only serious illness, which had happened seven years ago, had reappeared. For seven years he had been in the clear, and now, at the last moment . . . He rang his consultant (himself a keen walker and a very good friend to us) who immediately set all the bells ringing. On Monday morning, instead of catching the train, Eileen drove Herbert to the hospital where he had blood tests, X-rays and an examination under anaesthetic, at the end of which he was pronounced all clear. When Eileen went to collect him he was still in that state of fuzziness and generally chewed-about sort of feeling. 'Let's go tomorrow,' he said.

At long last we begin the diary which Eileen wrote up

meticulously three times a day in a series of red exercise books, which were the cheapest and lightest form of writing material we could find. We have resisted all temptations to edit it. It began as a series of notes rather than grammatical sentences, which perhaps was a reflection of the state of astonishment and wonderment in which we began the walk after so many months of preparation. It was difficult to believe it was really happening. But gradually the diary developed into more epic proportions as we realised it was the record of a journey of a lifetime. We also wondered whether to leave out all the family news, but again decided to let it stand as written. Although the various names will mean nothing to the reader, it is an indication that that little world which we had abandoned continued on its way without us. We were not indispensable.

Land's End

Land's End to John o' Groats

18th April to 2nd August 1991

16th April – Tuesday – 9.45 am

We're off – one day late. Comfortably seated in a first-class carriage by courtesy of British Rail. Our last minute hitch involved a day at the Sunderland Infirmary with tests, X-ray and an examination under a general anaesthetic. The miracle happened. Herbert was pronounced A1 and countdown recommenced.

9.00 pm – Land's End

The train ride was sheer joy as we went through England's green and pleasant land in brilliant sunshine. Crossing Brunel's Tamar Bridge was one of the highlights. Arriving at Land's End we were pleasantly surprised by the much criticised State House Hotel. Our bedroom and dining room are looking across to the Long Ships lighthouse bathed in the glow of the setting sun. Helen rang. And so to bed.

17th April – Wednesday

Rest day before the great trek begins. The taxi driver who brought us from Penzance asked us if we'd seen that film with Joss Ackland! Nearly a disaster – our new Panasonic camera went missing. Having searched the whole complex we gave it up as lost and went for a practice walk along the coastal path. The scenery is breathtaking – precipitous cliffs in some extraordinary shapes. The weather is perfect, sunny and windy, the sea shimmering like crystals, seagulls whirling overhead, pink, white and yellow flowers sprinkled along the cliff path like glowing jewels. We returned to the information office without much hope, only to be told our camera had been found and had been handed in to the hotel! O ye of little faith. Peter rang up at 9.00 pm.

18th April – Thursday – THIS IS THE DAY! Dry – dull – strong wind.

Day 1 – 5.00 pm

Today has gone off without a hitch – except for the near loss of our map due to high winds. The coastal path from Land's End has been spectacular. The sun came out and the sea became a brilliant turquoise. The Rev. John Davis, the local Christian Aid representative, saw us off after the statutory photographic session by the famous signpost (America 3,000 miles, John o' Groats 874 – that's by road. 1,100 for us). We had a short break at 1.00 pm for a sandwich and a drink, then up and down in the teeth of a Cornish gale. After walking for four hours we could still see the Land's End Hotel. Our first port of call is Botallack and we are overnighting at the Manor House Farm. A comfortable bedroom, the landlady is friendly but unfortunately no evening meal so we're off now (6.00 pm) to the local pub.

Oh dear – no food at the inn! On our return to the B & B our hostess took pity on us and ran us to the next village where we were regaled with steak and kidney pie, french onion soup and pud. Landlady picked us up at 8.15 pm. Bitterly cold night and our 'evening wear' is *very* thin. Early to bed.

Day 2 – 19th April, Friday

9.30 am. Just about to set off. Herbert is ringing Newquay about accommodation. Breakfast at the Manor Farm was marvellous. Fruit salad, any variety you wanted of bacon, egg etc., homemade brown bread and homemade marmalade. Met a young couple from Australia (they are English), he a lecturer in geology. They envied us. He was blond, extrovert, bursting with confidence. She was like a timid little brown mouse.

4.00 pm. We have been battling against strong northerly headwinds all day which pounded us unremittingly. An aged local told us it had been blowing for two weeks and would probably accompany us to Scotland. Very little sustenance today. The pub where we stopped for a respite produced only crisps and cider (and a bar of chocolate) but the walk was stimulating. We avoided the coastal path which, although dramatic, would have nearly doubled the distance. Instead we did a mixture of minor roads, interspersed with footpaths across fields – always in sight of the blue Atlantic. In spite of the cold wind the sun shone most of the day. The cows are all a deep golden brown and we saw a field full of very contented grazing pigs.

We are staying overnight at St Ives – a typical seaside resort. Our B & B is one of hundreds of identical ones. It is quite different from our previous overnight stops, but very clean and the landlady is smiling and friendly. The evening meal costs £4. What will we get to eat for £4? Herbert asks. Today I fell into a bog and got covered in mud. 'Typical,' said Herbert! I hope it will brush off as I have only one pair of walking trousers.

The inexpensive meal was a revelation. Chicken soup (piping hot), plaice and chips, beautifully presented, and chocolate gateau. We are fortunate people. Rang Peter as there was no reply from Jane (our communicator).

9.25 pm bed! (12 miles today).

Population of St Ives – winter 8,000, summer 80,000.

Exchanging pleasantries with a couple from Guildford at breakfast, the wife, on hearing we were walkers from Northumberland, remarked with a smile 'Well I don't suppose you'll be walking back to Northumberland'. 'No, a lot further.' Terry, our hostess is a native of Wales. Always smiling, always talking, always enjoying life (even though

The Diarist

she works 14 hours a day in the season). The top drawer. We promised to send her a postcard when we finished.

Day 3 – 20th April – Saturday

The wind has died down thank goodness. The sun has been shining all day, but we are both very tired tonight. The third day, we have been told, is always difficult. Our route has been mainly on road, but we went on the coastal path now and then. The Cornish Arms at Hayle provided a sandwich for our lunch, also a lonely old lady who attached herself to us, drank one brandy after another and told us her life history. We are now at Port Reith. Like the other B & Bs, it is spotlessly clean, but a bit cheerless. So we are spending the evening in the local pub, sitting beside a roaring fire (really gas). A wonderful meal has made us forget our tiredness.

Day 4 – 21st April – Sunday

Our route from Port Reith to Perronporth took us over the coastal path once more. It was a marvellous cliff walk with only the seagulls for company. We'd heard there were very few B & Bs here so are staying at the only hotel. No meal unfortunately so have to rely on the local again.

6.00 pm. Off to church now.

7.00 pm. After being directed to the Catholic church, we eventually found the Methodist. A very grand building – but quite empty of people! So we are now sitting in 'The Cottage Grill' eating fish and chips.

Day 5 – 22nd April – Monday

This hotel is a place where we wipe the dust off our feet. Soggy bed – we ended up sleeping on the floor – plastic flowers and plastic bottles of tomato sauce on the tables, pop music blasting our eardrums. In the entrance hall is a notice, 'If you liked your stay tell others, if you didn't tell us.' We did, but they weren't interested. Never mind – we'll get all sorts, and the others have been good.

Day 5 has dawned fine and clear after a very windy night. It is still chilly. From our window we can see the huge sandy bay which we will soon be walking across. The Atlantic breakers are rolling ceaselessly onward. Now we're off to Newquay.

After slithering and sliding up and down sand dunes we began our high altitude walking once again. A notice written by the Cornish County Council told us that the cliff path we were about to tackle was 'long and arduous' and that there were 'no toilet facilities or refreshments'. It ended with the words 'enjoy your walk'. Well, we certainly did. The scenery compensated for the difficulties. Again we've had a breezy, sunny day which has been ideal walking weather. We began to wilt about 1.00 pm but found a pub which gave us wholemeal sandwiches and coffee. As usual it took us longer to reach our destination than planned, but at Newquay the Tourist Information people fixed us up with a bed and breakfast. So here we are in a house which couldn't be more different from our miserable experience last night. Our hostess is kind and welcoming. We have a spacious bedroom – en suite what's more – and there's a marvellous smell coming from the kitchen. We aren't being pushed out tonight. This is 'The Alex' at Porth. Our hostess is Mrs Matthews. Over dinner, which was excellent, we got chatting with another couple (about our age). He was ex-RAF, and he talked about his experiences in Singapore, Germany and Ireland. It's the people you meet that make this trip so fascinating.

Now I'm sitting beside a huge window watching the sun setting over the Atlantic Ocean.

Day 6 – 23rd April – Tuesday Dull but dry; but we hope – it will get out.

We continued our friendship with the RAF couple over breakfast. Both aged 69. So now we're packing up and setting off for Padstow – 10 miles away.

Actually it was 13. We walked the first part of our journey on the cliffs, then on road past a derelict airfield. We decided to walk on minor roads and sadly there were no pubs or cafes – so no lunch. It was very cold. We had a few raisins and some dextrosol, and at St Merryon we found a pub where we persuaded the landlord, who was just about to close as it was after 3 o'clock, to give us some tea which revived us. Then off again on the final two miles to Padstow. Our B & B is very pleasant. There's a bath which is a great luxury. The present water shortage in Cornwall is so acute that people are usually expected to take showers.

It is now 6.30 pm and we are in the London Inn waiting (until 7) for a meal. We hate turning out again when we have finished walking for the day but most B & Bs don't do an evening meal. The landlord of the pub where we had our welcome cup of tea today asked us where we'd walked from. 'From Newquay.' 'My God!' he exclaimed.

Walking on these narrow roads with high hedges walkers are in great danger of sudden death from fast-moving traffic which comes whizzing round the bends. Luckily so far we've survived! We spoke to Helen using the phone card she gave us. They moved into their extension today.

A large group of very noisy people – all women except for three men – have just squeezed into the tiny pub and it was obvious they needed our table. As we got up to leave I said to one of the men, 'The local art club?' 'No – guess again.' It turned out the men were from the Cammelford Rotary Club and were treating the women to dinner as they'd been raising money for cancer research by a sponsored cycle ride. Herbert promptly gave them £5, and when they heard of our project one of the Rotarians returned the compliment and gave £5 to Christian Aid.

Day 7 – 24th April – Wednesday Cloudy (rain during night). Looks showery, but quite bright.

We've had a marvellous night – very good bed, excellent breakfast. We are very blessed. Short day today – we are going shopping for iron rations so we aren't caught out as we were yesterday.

2.30 pm. Here we are at Port Isaac. We've only done 7 miles today and have just booked in at the School House Hotel as there were no B & Bs to be seen.

Time to reminisce. Our overnight stay yesterday was quite extraordinary. Our bedroom was the ultimate in luxury – unlike this very much more expensive pad where we are now. Salmon pink satin cushions, curtains and lampshade. Masses of knick-knacks such as china ducks, frogs, birds, etc. A huge double bath with a fancy design and elaborate gold bathroom fittings. On another tack the public footpaths were disastrous yesterday. The farmer had pre-empted walkers' rights of way with barbed wire and electric fences and we had to retrace our steps – always a depressing experience.

(Pause while we enjoy our first Cornish cream tea. We had no lunch today).

Today the farmers have been more considerate and we were able to get off the roads onto footpaths from time to time. The highlight of the day was undoubtedly the ferry across the estuary – without it we would have had an extra

14 miles to walk. We had to 'walk the plank' when disembarking and the ferryman held our hands to prevent us from falling. Before going on the ferry we had a long chat with an old Cornishman in a little shop by Padstow's waterfront. The harbour is unspoilt, with fishing boats plying in and out, lobster pots on the quayside, and quaint old houses alongside all higgledepiggledy.

Port Isaac too is what every tourist imagines a Cornish village to be – if you discount the rows of modern houses on the cliff tops. The narrow road, indeed the only road, winds steeply down to the harbour, and then winds as steeply up again. The tiny cottages (which sadly don't seem to have heard of bed and breakfast) are all different, seem very old and are mostly whitewashed.

Day 8 – 25th April – Thursday

This hotel was a school for 100 years, and the dining room was the old assembly hall. It's an amazing place, rather like a baronial hall. It has a high raftered ceiling and heraldic crests and deer heads decorate the walls. High standard of food and good service. They dried our socks last night. The weather looks threatening today. Wind still northerly, temperature 10 degrees. So we'll put on all our woollies and hope for the best. We will start off along the coastal path and see how far we get. We have nothing booked for tonight.

Spoke to Jane last night. She will post our first map replacements to Bideford where we are booked in at a Ramblers' hotel. We tried out her miniature Scrabble last night which was great fun. The bed was *very* hard.

The proprietress of the School House Hotel, on being asked to sign our verification form, unhesitatingly handed over £10 for Christian Aid. She talked about the hotel and said she usually had 'nice' people staying (like us presumably!). Certainly there was no pop music, fruit machines or tomato sauce in plastic bottles, but there were also very few people there so she may be fighting a losing battle.

4.30 pm. After a very strenuous day we have arrived in Tintagel. We had to abandon the coastal path after some really gruelling ups and downs. The cliffs are beautiful, precipitous and very slow going. The road (which we had great difficulty in finding due to overgrown footpaths and barbed wire) was less interesting but very quick. So now we are established in a basic B & B. But at least there is a bath and a meal so we have a lot to be thankful for. Herbert is a bit depressed – feels he's making a mess of the planning, but actually he's doing magnificently.

We met a pleasant couple on the cliffs who live in Tiverton in Devon. They talked about the water problem which has reached crisis point down here. The planners seem to have got it all wrong. There were floods a few years ago so they provided escape routes for the water and now what little there is just runs away. We've just finished a perfectly lovely meal – all homemade. We get the most unexpected surprises on this trip.

Bedtime – 8.10 pm.

Day 9 – 26th April – Friday A clear bright morning.

We're going to have a look at King Arthur's castle before setting off this morning. Then it is 10 miles to Crackington. Very nice people running this B & B. Came from Birmingham a year ago.

The morning has been hard work – up and down the coastal path – but as we approached Bos Castle the coastline became more and more dramatic. We climbed high and looked downwards hundreds of feet at the foaming waves beating against the rocks, the gulls wheeling and soaring far below us, and wild flowers of every colour surrounding us. We passed a young couple, each with a baby on their backs and we felt they were more heavily laden than we were. Sadly we were once more forced to leave these marvellous cliffs as the mountaineering with our heavy packs became too exhausting. We stopped for a welcome glass of milk and a sandwich at a quaint little coffee shop – run by a young man wearing the Star of David. He told us he had served 16,000 cream teas last summer.

The afternoon was also hard work but we made quicker

progress. We were on road and the first four miles were uphill which was a great effort. After about 7 miles we arrived at Coombe Barton Inn at Crackington. We are right in the cove and can see – and hear – the sea from our bedroom. It is much more luxurious than last night – and we have our own bath. As we are both completely jiggered we are very grateful for the comfort. We'll go back to simplicity tomorrow. Herbert rang the Ramblers' place in Bideford to say we'd be there on Monday instead of Sunday as we'd lost time on the coastal paths. (The first $1\frac{1}{2}$ miles this morning took us 3 hours.) The proprietor told us our parcel had arrived. Thank you Jane!

I'm sitting beside the window of our room and can see the 200 ft sheer cliff up which the coastal path goes from here – so it will be the road again probably. If we stayed on the coast we'd never get out of Cornwall.

Digression to Tintagel and King Arthur. The place is entirely dependent upon King Arthur. Everything is King Arthur's, Merlin's, Camelot's. We had tea at a roadside cafe called Excalibur. So before we left we went down the ritual path which the elderly, the crippled, the overweight all staggered down to see the sacred relics. It was an impressive position, but from what we could see from lower down, not particularly interesting. There were remains on the mainland as well as the 'island'. As it was English Heritage (which means we pay) and a fairly lengthy diversion we didn't go up. But we did go into the exhibition which told us that King Arthur – if there ever was a King Arthur – didn't come here, that it was a legend invented by someone called Mortimer, a pal of Henry VIII, that the present buildings were 12–13th century and that eventually they will disappear into the sea.

Day 10 – 27th April – Saturday Coombe Barton, Crackington. A beautiful morning – not a cloud.

Our night's rest was somewhat disturbed by a noisy disco just beneath us, but the bed was comfy and the room spacious. Herbert spoke to Heather. They are planning to join us somewhere next week, but she was vague about details. More roadwork today. Never mind, we have the prospect of long distance footpaths ahead. Grapefruit (genuine variety) and honey for breakfast, also a marvellous view of the sea.

Yesterday we were excited to see a large sign by the roadside. Desperate for a drink we hurried towards it. What did it say? 'Free manure.'

4.00 pm. We have just settled in at the local pub at Stratton. This is an inland village as we decided to bypass Bude to save a mile tomorrow. This morning we left Crackington by road, but went back to the coastal path before long as it was our last day beside the blue Atlantic. We stopped at a surf bathers' beach and had our first Cornish pasty. Very tasty! Herbert took pictures of sea pinks which grow in gay abandon on the cliffs. To our dismay, just as we turned for a last glimpse of the glorious scene which had accompanied us for ten days, we saw a group of elderly people struggling to pick up litter which was scattered all over the steep cliffs. We felt we should have stayed to help them, but time was pressing. There do not seem to be any B & Bs here and the innkeeper wasn't keen to have us as they were renovating, but she took pity on us. We may have looked a bit pathetic. We are in a 13th century inn 'The Tree'. We have had to cross a courtyard to the bar for our supper – a part of the building even older, 11th century. There is a roaring log fire (genuine, not gas), old settles and ancient pieces of copper. All very picturesque, but the meal of fish and chips was disappointing.

9.15 pm bedtime.

Day 11 – 28th April – Sunday Fine and clear. Aren't we lucky? We are setting off into the unknown. No accommodation, just hoping for the best.

It's been a sunny day – an easy walk but less exciting than the coast. A happy surprise when we were getting hungry – upper Tamar Lake where there was sailing, windsurfing and, more useful to us, a little cafe. So we had a glass of milk, a sandwich and a banana. Arriving in Bradworthy we were told the only inn had no accommodation. Disaster – nowhere to sleep. But we obviously have a guardian angel as we found a B & B on the road out of the village. It's a converted barn – very attractive but rather cold. We were given a riotous welcome from the family. Bed? No problem. A meal? No problem at all. So here we are in the family sitting room in the company of two of the children – one asleep, the other glued to the telly.

Well, that was some meal! Nettle soup (with cream), spaghetti bolognaise, baked potatoes garnished with apples, cucumber, tomatoes, onion and mushroom. Bramble crumble and ice-cream. We are constantly being surprised. There are two girls, 12 and 13 – who waited at table (to earn pocket money), a baby of two and another on the way. What energy to run a B & B as well. Again tried to go to church. Again no service.

Day 12 – 29th April – Monday Rain.

We've got to know the family here. Keith, Ros, Gail, Dianne and 2-year-old Eleanor. Keith, a New Zealander. Second marriage. Two girls by first. Lovely people.

They are obviously having a struggle to make ends meet, but are generous in their provision for their guests. The snag is the temperature, but with the high roof it must cost a fortune to heat. A very romantic place.

12.30 pm. The Bell Inn, Parkham. We've been walking in rain for over two hours, and our new Peter Storm rainwear – guaranteed 100% waterproof – has let in water.

* * *

Reflections of Cornwall. Yesterday we crossed the Tamar into Devon. First and foremost our memories are of the soaring cliffs and crashing waves, flowers and sunshine, but in complete contrast we remember as well the rows of cheap-looking caravans and small modern housing estates, theme parks and all the trappings of modern tourism which seem to be competing against the wild natural beauty. But the natural world of sea, rocks, flowers and birds will remain long after the manmade incongruities have disappeared. At Land's End life seemed very primitive in sympathy with the landscape: the signs of civilisation were shabby and untidy, broken down cars and bedsteads as well as the derelict tin mines. It is an extension of England where the local inhabitants seem to have been left behind in the race for progress and where survival is a struggle. But it isn't long before you reach the pleasure-seeking set-up of today, and people in their 10s of 1000s come to enjoy themselves in the summer, which is now Cornwall's only means of existence.

Tin Mine

* * *

5.00 pm. Bideford. At last we have arrived at the Mount Hotel after continuous rain and two hours on the A39. It has undoubtedly been the worst day yet. In spite of our new rainwear we were both soaked to the skin. So we are asking Jane to send another parcel – our old Gore-tex which is much heavier, but hopefully more reliable. We've been on the road all day, but mostly minor ones which were quite pretty. A good bowl of hot soup revived us in the middle of the day, and a hot bath on arrival was a great comfort. We're hoping for a dry day tomorrow.

Two old ladies are the only other guests. One of them said

she'd seen our picture in a newspaper (possibly the Methodist Recorder) and wonder of wonders – the owners of the hotel, a married couple, brought a note into the lounge and laid it beside us. It read 'Mike and Janet Taylor would like to donate the cost of your visit to Christian Aid'. When we arrived at the door our hostess looked at the two dripping and bedraggled hikers and we asked her, 'Do you want us?' 'Not really', she replied. But we have received nothing but kindness from her and her husband.

Day 13 – 30th April – Tuesday

The rain has stopped at last, although it's inclined to be foggy. We've had a marvellous night's sleep, evening meal and breakfast. So now we are ready to do battle once more. Twelve miles to do today. A wonderful send-off by Mike and Janet, but no reply from the B & B at Umberleigh (our destination for today), so we just had to set off in faith once more. Herbert was given a cheque by one of the other guests. We shopped in Bideford – postcards, a comb and dextrosol, then began the 12-mile trek. Our host and hostess had given us an orange each which was just as well as we found nowhere to eat. We were on the narrow lanes which criss-cross Devon and which were completely unpopulated. Fortunately it stayed dry, but was dull and windy. The last stretch was on another A-road and we came across a Spar shop. A girl standing outside said, 'We open tomorrow'. Obviously things begin to happen by the 1st of May in Devon. The Tourist Board had told us there were lots of places to stay in Umberleigh. There were in fact two. The first either couldn't or wouldn't have us. Although at home, they didn't open the door. The second, 'The Rising Sun', has. So here we are, in a very pretty bedroom. It's 4.00 pm and the landlord has made us some cheese sandwiches which were most acceptable in view of our lunchless day. So although footsore we'll soon recover. Serendipity – an unexpected surprise of a pleasant nature. Wild life – a flock of flying geese overhead, otherwise only a couple of rabbits and a dead hedgehog (which could hardly be called life). Again it's the people you meet as much as the countryside who are making our walk so interesting. The kindness of our host and hostess last night was quite remarkable. Mike even offered to drive over here with our rucksacks, but as we had no accommodation booked that wasn't possible.

Day 14 – 1st May – Wednesday

Two lots of bad news last night. We heard from Peggie that Cecily had died. Poor Marjorie, she will be devastated. Could not get her on the phone. Also Peter and Heather have been told by Wimpey to move to Manchester. What an upheaval for them. But we press on. Today is, like yesterday, dry but dull. Herbert is as ever poring over the map, trying to work out the best route. It's hard labour for him. Last night at dinner (when we had poached salmon) the landlord told us that 'an elderly gentleman' had lunched here last week on his way to John o' Groats, also on foot. 'How elderly?' we enquired. 'About 64 I think', was the reply. Later he was identified as Douglas Phelps with white whiskers.

It is now 1.50 pm and we are another 7 miles nearer to our goal.

The road journey has been enlivened by a conversation with two old ladies who had parked their car in a lay-by to drink coffee – a conversation which would have lasted forever if we hadn't politely terminated it. Anyway, they offered us coffee and, much better, recommended a B & B in Taunton. The countryside is green with rolling hills on all sides. Innumerable cows – fat and contented – and sheep with lambs munching away. The hedgerows are ablaze with colour. I stooped to catch the scent of a beautiful purple flower like a miniature hyacinth, but sadly it could only afford a pretty dress, not perfume as well. We are now having a much needed rest in a 17th century inn in South Molton, awaiting our sandwiches. The going doesn't seem to get any easier and we are both tired after 3 hours walking. We must present a quaint spectacle when we arrive at our various hostelries. The proprietor of The Rising Sun last night looked very suspiciously at us when we asked for a room. How can these scruffy hikers expect to stay here, he seemed to be thinking. But as we so often find, we were the best of friends when we left this morning.

Our sandwiches today are a great improvement upon yesterday, when we ate half an orange each, sitting down in the road as the grass verges were too wet.

4.00 pm. Kerscott Farm. We had a pleasant hour with a lady in the Tourist Information Office at South Molton (where we'd had lunch) and we were fixed up with tonight's accommodation. It is quite a place. Absolutely chock-a-block with antiques of every description. As has so often been the situation, we are the only people staying here so we have a good opportunity to look around. There are huge fireplaces (with no heat, alas) made of stone with kettles, pans, bellows, brass plates etc., all hanging in the cavity round the black, unlit stoves. Every surface is covered with china ornaments, cut glass, expensive looking porcelain, antique chairs, grandfather clocks, aspidistras in enormous china bowls decorated with large pink roses, lace cloths, china dogs galore and at least four large cheese bells. The pictures are all Victorian and the whole effect is quite extraordinary. The farmer's wife is very kind and we've had a meal of soup, very tender roast beef and a tasty apple sponge and custard. I really don't know why, with so many valuable possessions, they need to take in visitors – perhaps they like the company as it's a very isolated place. We'll be going to bed soon to get warm.

Day 15 – 2nd May – Thursday

We have both slept well – after our toes and noses had unfrozen. Breakfast was disappointing. Like the house – the bacon and egg were cold. Our hostess bade us farewell while we were still breakfasting and went off to market, but we had a long chat with her husband, the farmer. Like many he was full of complaints about the state of the sheep market, but what really worried him was what had happened to the swallows? Only one had returned this year (we saw it on the telephone wire). Last year he had 25. He was convinced the world was drifting into crisis. He then started reminiscing about his past guests – now less numerous because the road numbers had all changed and they were no longer on the A361. He used to get exciting foreigners, now only boring old English turned up. (We apologised for our unfortunate nationality.) He remembered particularly the four American ladies – 'hilarious they were' – who'd got through 13 husbands between them, and as they killed them off they got richer and richer. How Americans stood the temperature in the farm we couldn't imagine. He'd really got into the swing of things when he heard the phone ringing (exciting foreigners perhaps), so with a hurried 'I'll talk to you later', he ran indoors and we escaped. Our route – all on road – was much pleasanter than the previous two days. Firstly the sun was shining and secondly we were no longer in enclosed little lanes but on a high level road from which we could see for miles over the green countryside. As time went on we were buoyed up with the prospect of a post office which appeared on our OS map after six miles. But as so often has happened in Devon it was unable to supply our – very simple – needs. We wanted a drink, they sold newspapers and stamps. A little further along another notice informed us we could buy calor gas. So we trudged on and on until – after nine miles – we came to an inn. We were welcomed warmly by the proprietor who said she'd passed us on the road (she'd been playing golf). We told her where we were bound tonight and were heartened to hear that the inn, which was quite posh, sent overflow visitors there. 'You'll be very relaxed with Peter and Cindy,' she told us. So here we are in another farm which the Tourist Office kindly booked for us without charge.

The contrast with last night could not be greater. It is a most beautiful house and garden. Everything is tasteful and comfortable and, thank goodness, WARM. There is a luxurious bathroom but because of the water crisis we were asked not to use the bath, just the shower, but it's such a lovely place we don't even mind that. (At Kerscott the bath was covered over with a board and more enormous ornaments placed on top so that it was impossible to use it anyway). This farm is organic, and as we're both heartily sick of fried breakfasts we're hoping to be given some fruit.

The view from our bedroom window at last gives us a sight of Devon as we imagined it. Very green and curvaceous with more dramatic scenery than we have sighted so far in this county: it is overlooking the Exe valley which runs through the steep gorge in the middle distance. We both agree we wouldn't mind staying here a second night but we are already booked up tomorrow (despite gloomy predictions by the Tourist Information) and have to meet Peter and family on the road into Taunton on Saturday. We are nearly out of Devon. So far we have known it only for cold winds and grey skies (and primroses). But this is a much more attractive picture.

Day 16 – 3rd May – Friday

Our stay at Rows Farm has been one of the most memorable so far. Our hostess, Cindy, not only cooked us a very good meal, but spent the evening chatting to us. The sitting room overlooked the sloping, colourful garden and the rolling Devon hills beyond. The house is 17th century and very tastefully furnished. Peter used to be a policeman and they have come from Barnet in Hertfordshire. The story of how they came to Devon is quite romantic. They used to holiday here in a caravan and got to know the couple who owned Rows Farm. Cindy and Peter helped them renovate the old house. The husband died suddenly and after a year his widow, who was crippled, could no longer manage it on her own, so it was put on the market. After a lot of negotiation, plus a miracle which involved the discovery of some banknotes under the floorboards of their house, they managed to buy the house in which they'd worked so hard and which they had fallen in love with. Cindy has a full-time job as well as running the guest house. Peter used to supply organic vegetables but that folded up so he is now a general factotum about the place, doing whatever needs doing. He's also an artist, which was a great excitement for Herbert. They had an enormous collection of books – any of which we were welcome to read – and altogether we had a very happy time with them. Breakfast at our request was rolls, cereal and fruit.

It is difficult not to make a comparison between the two farms of the two consecutive nights. Kerscott was a monument to the past, with its Victorian pictures, ornaments and clocks which had stopped probably years ago. Both the farmer and his wife were recalling the good times which had ended – the decline in demand for sheep, the lack of guests because of the new road. All negative. Cindy and Peter were looking forward. Despite the failure of his organic vegetable enterprise, they were courageously facing one exciting challenge after another. They were on the same road as the people at Kerscott Farm, but were just looking for ways to overcome their difficulties. They were a pleasure to meet.

We have continued on the B3227 this morning, and having bought our lunch in Bampton (a beautiful little town) we've stopped – at 12.30 pm – to eat it in order to reduce the weight in our packs. Sitting on a seat which we had first to divest of brambles. (We rang Hill Rise last night. Helen out, but Herbert had a long talk with Rob. He's being sent out to Australia on Saturday. Everything happens when we go away it seems.) Opposite the bench where we are having our lunch is a notice pointing the way to a 'Dried Flower Shop'. I am often reminded on this trip of a saying by Thomas Carlyle, 'The world is full of things I do not want' – like free manure, calor gas, stamps, and now dried flowers.

After a long hike along the B3227 – much refreshed by our picnic – we arrived at the steep turn-off to our B & B for tonight. We were in luck. There was a farm shop offering cream teas, so of course we couldn't refuse an offer like that. This was our first experience of clotted cream which was enhanced by the feather-light scones and, wonder of wonders, tea with leaves instead of bags. Then it was up and up until we were 750 feet above sea level with wonderful views all round us. We'd passed the boundary into Somerset about an hour before and we both noticed a change. The countryside was softer and gentler, the houses more mellow and the cattle even more contented looking. Our arrival at North

Down Farm was greeted by a smiling young farmer's wife who led us upstairs into a veritable Aladdin's cave of treasures. Our bedroom could not be surpassed by a 5-star hotel. We have in fact two rooms and a third which has a loo and washbasin. The suite – for that is what it is – is decorated in Delft blue, everything matching from the frilly bed covers and cushions to the curtains, wallpaper, lampshade and carpet, and everything brand new. As if this wasn't enough we were then shown the bathroom. Pink this time. Gold taps etc. Mahogany cupboards, loo seat and bath surround. Thick carpet, elaborate shower, tiles with flower designs and cottage pink wallpaper. We have yet to see the downstairs. (Douglas Phelps stayed here last week so we're obviously following him. He arrived puffing.)

* * *

Reflections of Devon. As we leave Devon and journey on into Somerset, perhaps the predominant impression is of the masses of wild primroses in the hedgerows, and of the many miles of tiny lanes with their high, dense hedges. The weather was disappointing for some of our walk through Devon, but it is the great kindness we received from so many people there which will remain with us. Cindy and Peter gave us £5 for Christian Aid and asked us to let them know when we reach our goal. They have a hard road ahead and we wish them well.

* * *

At North Down Farm. We had another marvellous meal, roast beef from one of their own bullocks. Afterwards we sat alone in the rather chilly room, which was a bit of a let down after the exotic upper floor, because the farmer and his wife were busy entertaining (exciting?) French visitors. A good night, with a good bed. Beds, we are quickly discovering, are a very important matter for long distance walkers. Too soft and your back aches, too hard and your back aches!

Day 17 – 4th May – Saturday Dull, wet, cold.

Herbert spoke to Peter last night. They'll meet us somewhere along the B3227. It's a shame the weather is so poor for their brief holiday. They were a bit cast down after an abortive househunting mission in Manchester. But these things don't happen in a hurry.

We have continued along our old friend the B3227 but have been enjoying the Somerset countryside with the red soil, green meadows, flowering trees and attractive red brick architecture. After a breakfast of fruit, yoghurt, toast and marmalade we bade farewell to our kind hostess – Lucy – and her French guests and set off downhill towards Wiveliscombe. This little town is not quite as attractive as Bampton (which is a real gem), but is a nice little place. Herbert took a photograph of an Elizabethan building which dominated the main street. We were on the lookout for Peter and family but as we hadn't met them by 1.00 pm we stopped for our usual cider and cheese sandwich. By mistake I opened the door marked 'Bar' not 'Lounge'. Inside was scruffy, and the clientele entirely male. We sat down as unobtrusively as we could and listened to their conversation. They obviously all knew each other, and it was a joy to listen to the incomprehensible rolling Somerset dialect. Before we left they started talking to us and discovered what we were doing. They all wished us well. (There was another trace of the mysterious Douglas Phelps.)

So on and on and on we walked until, quite suddenly, there appeared in a lay-by five cyclists setting off down the dangerous road. The younger Witheringtons had arrived. We all sat down on the grass for about half an hour exchanging news, then we set off for Taunton, minus our rucksacks which were given the treat, not allowed to us, of travelling in a car. We covered the remaining 4 miles quite fast, unencumbered with our usual burden. Arriving at our B & B (next door to Sainsburys with a view over the car park) we were dismayed to discover that our rucksacks – containing all our worldly goods – had not arrived. To say we felt vulnerable is an understatement. Whatever had happened? It should have taken Peter only 10 minutes to drive from the lay-by to Taunton and the walk was 1½ hours. We sat in our room – which was warm, but a dreadful conglomeration of colours – and waited and waited and waited. Eventually the doorbell rang, and our agony ended. The family had got no reply when they first arrived. The landlady was out. So they had taken the children swimming. How thankful we are to have some clean clothes, also some different waterproofs, lent by Helen. We unloaded our dirty washing on to Heather, who will send it off clean to Jane. How very kind our children are.

When we'd washed and changed we all had a meal together in a nearby Berni Steak House to celebrate Peter's 40th birthday. The company was better than the meal.

9.00 pm. Goodnight.

Day 18 – 5th May – Sunday Bank Holiday weekend.

A good night – although the party at the County Hotel next door was noisy. We have requested no cooked breakfast and our hostess has suggested tinned fruit. Here we are back to plastic flowers and pop music, masses of brass ornaments and plastic tablecloths as well. But you can't win them all. The little backyard beneath our window is festooned with plastic gnomes, dogs and cats – and beyond is the car park of the opulent County Hotel – the boundary between rich and poor being an old brick wall. Our hostess has been very interested in our gear. As Herbert was paying the bill I put on my rucksack. 'Is it heavy?' she asked. 'Yes', I replied. 'Well why don't 'e carry it then?' she said indignantly.

This morning is again dull, but fortunately dry. We soon left Taunton (without regret as it was just another over-crowded town full of the usual chain shops) and walked first on A roads and then country lanes. The village of Ham was a picturebook hamlet – untouched by modern civilisation. Flowering cherry, ceanothis, almond and weeping willow, wallflowers, broom and wisteria tumbling everywhere in scented profusion. A dream world.

At 12.30 pm we saw a sign to 'The Rising Sun' at Lower Knapp, so we left our route and trudged downwards in search of sustenance. A VERY POSH place – what a contrast to the public bar yesterday. Huge log fire and velvet seats. We ordered a ploughman's lunch as there were no sandwiches on Sundays. There was such a huge piece of cheese we wondered whether we dared put the surplus in our bags, but it was whisked away before we had an opportunity.

This 'Rising Sun' reminds us of the last Rising Sun where we had such a happy time. In the dining room there the only other guest – a young man working in the area – told us some interesting facts about the local art of thatching. There are many thatched roofs in the West Country and we were told of one house which had recently been rethatched at a cost of £29,000. Also that there was a four-year waiting list. A very special type of straw is used, and of course the thatching itself is a very skilled craft.

Back to the present. Most of the clientele of this hostelry are very upper class English gentlemen and ladies, but there's an extraordinary quartet sitting beside us. Two elderly ladies and what I can only describe as two gigolos. If only we knew their story!

4.15 pm. After a walk of 1½ hours along the leafy Somerset lanes and villages with no sign of B & Bs, suddenly we saw one, 'The Jays Nest'. Here we are in a wonderful country house hotel. We were welcomed with open arms, given tea and biscuits by the proprietor, who asked us lots of questions about our journey. Now we are bathed – lashings of hot water for a change – dressed in our 'evening clothes' and sitting in a sunny room overlooking a colourful garden. There's a dovecot with its inmates flying in and out, and a snowy white cat on the chair beside us. A large apple tree in full bloom outside the window completes the picture of peaceful beauty. Our hostess has promised us a meal, but first we are going to the local Parish church. Yes, there really is a service tonight.

What fun! The vicar said he'd read about us in the local Christian Aid magazine. A fine old church, but there were only seven in the congregation (including the two booted walkers).

We've just had another Egon-Ronay style meal. Really we are so lucky. Again we are staying in a lovely house, on our own except for one young couple.

10.00 pm. We've been talking so long to Jane and Helen

that I fear we have kept our hosts waiting to lock up. Jane spoke about Cecily's funeral and how upset Marjorie was. Jane had also been to Langley Park to see Grandma – bless her heart.

The Jay's Nest

Day 19 – 6th May – Monday A wonderful morning.

We learnt last night that this house is called 'The Jay's Nest' because everyone's name begins with 'J'. Including the cat's.

We are sitting beside the window looking out over the garden and to the fields beyond. Somerset is an enchanting county. This is a B & B we'll be very sorry to leave. Over breakfast Jayne told us her life story, which is something which happens to us repeatedly on our travels. She'd been an England hockey player and also a rep. driving 40,000 miles a year, the combination of these having caused severe foot troubles. She'd had five operations on her feet – one of which had made the condition worse. She had been widowed and Bill (he doesn't begin with 'J'), the gentleman who seemed to do everything, was her business partner, not her husband as we'd thought. Another act of generosity – Jayne refused to take Herbert's cheque. 'My donation to Christian Aid', she said. What kind people we are meeting!

We bade them farewell – also the young couple who were staying there – and wended our way through the dreamy, sunny countryside to the accompaniment of birdsong, the scent of lilac and apple blossom, and at one point the thunder of the 125 roaring along the mainline. We continue to see notices advising us we can buy what we certainly do not want. This time we were offered budgies, geese and ducklings. We'd told Peter we would be at the post office in Lamport at 1.00 pm and we waited in a filthy car park, full of litter and noisy motorcyclists in this disappointing town from 12.30 pm. Just as we were leaving, the red car with its five bicycles attached turned up. A Spar shop was open, even though it was bank holiday, so we bought some food and Peter and Heather drove off to find a picnic spot, followed by Eileen and Herbert, also Erica and Laurence who were very pleased to be part of the walk. They even tried carrying our haversacks for a few minutes. We had hot soup and tea as well as lots of goodies. We stayed too long, and it was 3.15 pm before we got going again. The children and Heather rode their bicycles beside us for a while. After we parted from them we found we'd missed our turning and had to retrace our steps which was a bit frustrating when we had so far to go, and the afternoon became quite a drag. We seemed to be walking for hours across uncharted countryside, following the Somerset Way and getting nowhere. It was nearly 5.30 pm and we had nowhere to sleep. It was still two miles to Street, which had been our intended destination. There was a village before Street called Dunden, and we were hoping to find something there. But all we could see were private houses. Then, round a corner, when all hope had gone, there appeared the longed-for sign – B & B! It is strange how this miracle has happened the last two nights and here we are – in bed at 7.45 pm. We are in what I can only describe as a country motel. Some stables have been converted into bedrooms, and you walk across a courtyard to an old stone cottage to eat. That is another miracle. When we staggered across the road in response to the sign and knocked at the door, the owner said, 'Yes', we could have a bed, but 'No', there was nothing to eat. I am ashamed to say Herbert pleaded with him, so he went in to see his wife and returned with the welcome news that she would make us an omelette. We bathed, changed and presented ourselves at the cottage and were shown into an attractive dining room where a table was laid for us. There we were regaled with homemade soup, a mushroom omelette with a salad and cherry pie with cream. I never cease to marvel at the change in our fortunes. As Gladys (from the Himalayan trip) used to say, 'Life is made up of contrasts'. One moment we are struggling along, tired, hungry and homeless: the next we are enjoying the luxury of a hot bath, with the prospect of a meal and a comfy bed. So we must have no fear of tomorrow.

Day 20 – 7th May – Tuesday

Dunden. Our unexpected refuge last night was another of our great treats. We had prunes and apricots for breakfast as well as the usual repast. Unbeknown to Herbert, however, during the night I developed a severe pain in my right arm, so severe that I could not lift it. What would happen in the morning? I asked myself in a panic. What if I couldn't carry my rucksack? This anxiety caused some sleepless hours, but when morning came I decided to say nothing, put on my rucksack and hope for the best. Gradually as I walked the pain lessened, until 24 hours later it disappeared for good. I will never know what had caused this alarming disability but I said a little prayer of gratitude that it had not prevented me from continuing the task we had set ourselves to do.

Our host and hostess at Dunden were, as we've found all along, both kind and generous – they said we should give the cost of our meal last night to Christian Aid. They joined us for breakfast and we learned that there is a large deer population in the area – disappointingly unseen by us. Our host had a number on his hill farm and recently had to shoot one of them which was ailing, in order to keep the rest healthy. We asked whether the men with guns we'd seen the previous day were after rabbits, but were told it was deer, which seemed to us to be rather sad; apparently they have to be culled regularly. This was another place we were sorry to leave.

It was raining as we set off, so we had a chance to try out

Helen's Gore-tex (no complaints). There was a long, steep hill to climb to Street, then we were quickly into Glastonbury. Now it is 1.20 pm and we are enjoying our daily swig of local cider, which is very potent, and a sandwich. We photographed the ruined abbey, but Glastonbury just seems to be the usual busy, overcrowded town. We prefer the country villages.

5.45 pm. We have arrived in Wells. As we had no accommodation we visited the Tourist Office who have found us a B & B bang in the centre of the city. We have to go out to eat unfortunately. Earlier we had passed a very attractive hotel with a vineyard attached but it was closed. Also a pretty farmhouse which would give us a bed but no food. So we pressed on.

This is a real character building. Our bedroom overlooks a little garden surrounded by tall trees so thick that you don't realise you are in the middle of a busy city. The bedroom is clean and festooned with rosebuds on bed, walls and curtains. The hall and staircase on the other hand look shabby and far from clean. Mine host is friendly and cheerful and I'm sure we'll have a good night's sleep. We are both ready for a day off after three weeks' non-stop walking so will stay two nights in Bath. Our landlord recommended his favourite pub which we looked at, then went elsewhere and had a good steak and kidney pie in a less pretentious and cheaper place. Tomorrow we'll have a look at the cathedral before moving off. It looks very impressive, although no good for a photograph as much of the facade is covered with scaffolding.

9.00 pm. Goodnight.

* * *

The Nature of Miracles

If you are reading the diary diligently you will have come across the word 'miracle'. This, of course, was written in the heat of the moment, when the experience was still fresh and full of wonder. Perhaps you may be thinking that while we were correcting mistakes in the diary and crossing out all the exclamation marks which punctuated the original pages, we should have taken the opportunity of watering down such emotive language. But we have left the miracles alone because they were part and parcel of our experiences over three months. When you undertake a marathon such as this, inevitably it means that you stretch your own resources, mental and physical, to the limit and beyond the limit. Such is the effect when your reach exceeds your grasp (we are always quoting this bit of Browning). Again and again you are dependent upon that helping hand to pull you through either the Slough of Despond or the more familiar sloughs which you meet, for instance, on the Pennine Way.

On one of the very early days – we can't recall which particular incident prompted it – we were reminded of a story told to us by a Scottish friend some years ago. It was told with some diffidence, we should add, in case it offended any theological sensitivity that we might suffer from. Far from it! We have always thought of it as the epitome of theological good sense. So here it is. It is about a Scottish priest (probably because it was told by our Scottish friend: no doubt he could equally well have been English, Irish or Welsh), who went out fishing one day in a little boat. He had rowed his boat some distance out to sea when a storm suddenly sprang up. The priest reminded himself of the storm on the lake in the Gospel when Jesus rebuked his disciples for being afraid and for their lack of faith; and he determined that he was not going to be afraid and that he was going to trust in the Lord. So when a fishing boat turned up and the skipper offered to tow his little boat back into port the priest waved him away. 'No, No!' he shouted back. 'My trust is in the Lord.' The fishing boat sailed away and the storm grew worse. A short while later a destroyer steamed up and the crew lowered a rope ladder down the side. 'Get hold of the ladder,' they shouted, 'and we'll rescue you.' 'No, no!' protested the priest. 'My trust is in the Lord.' So the destroyer sailed away and the storm grew worse and worse, until the little boat was full of water. All of a sudden, out of the sky appeared a helicopter which hovered over the boat. A voice called to him over the loud hailer, 'We're letting the harness down, get into it and we'll save you.' But the priest again waved it away. 'No, no!' he shouted above the noises of the storm and the helicopter. 'My trust is in the Lord.' The helicopter flew away; the storm grew worse; the little boat sank; the priest drowned. Later that day, as he was entering the pearly gates, he was welcomed by St Peter who noticed that he didn't have that usual radiant smile you expect on anyone who is entering Heaven, and he enquired if there was anything wrong. The priest replied in a rather disgruntled tone of voice, that there was a question he wanted to ask the Lord. 'That can be arranged,' said Peter, and the priest was shown into the presence of the Lord and told to ask his question. 'Why is it, Lord,' asked the priest, 'that when I trusted you to save me in the storm you allowed me to drown?' 'What do you mean, I allowed you to drown?' replied the Lord. 'Didn't I send you a fishing boat, and a destroyer, and a helicopter?'

That story was repeated day after day during our walk. In our need we found ourselves looking for the fishing boat and the destroyer and the helicopter, and identifying them when they came along. Which they always did.

* * *

Day 21 – (3 weeks) – 8th May – Wednesday Dull, cold, dry.

Our overnight stay was quite romantic after all. The house had a door directly onto the busy city centre. You entered a narrow hall and this widened into a vast area with rooms going on and on backwards. It is a 17th century house built on the site of a 14th century building. The only other person staying was a retired clergyman who was a permanent resident. He'd separated from his wife – 'the duchess' – and eight children, and had bed and breakfasted for five years in 'Richmond House', going out every night to a restaurant for a meal – a pathetic existence. The landlord looked like a funny little gnome or leprechaun. He was very chatty. Talked about the Cathedral which had no bishop at the moment, and his wife who was in Canada visiting grandchildren.

Before leaving Wells we booked tonight's accommodation, then went to see the Bishop's Palace which is surrounded by a moat and drawbridge, and also the 12th century Cathedral. There are 700 carved figures on the facade of this great building. A scissors arch was added in the 14th century to buttress the tower which was sinking. Christ on the Cross dominates the nave with carved figures on either side. The vaulted ceiling is plastered and decorated with old floral designs. As a communion service was taking place we were asked not to wander around.

10.30 am. Left Wells and climbed (on minor roads) the Mendip Hills. An easy walk led us to Binegar where, at the 'Horse and Jockey', we had a toasted sandwich. Asked if we'd like 'the rough stuff' we felt it wise to decline.

On our way up to Binegar we crossed an old railway line (twice) – presumably S & DJR – climbing up the Mendips to 750 ft then across the plateau. The Station House, almost lost in the undergrowth which has taken over the railway, was a

Wells

private house. What makes these old railways so romantic when they were noisy, cold, dirty, late? Probably the great spirit of adventure (commercial adventure) which inspired the early engineers to overcome the contours, valleys, rivers, rock, forest. What will it be like when the roads are unused and taken over again by nature?

At the 'Horse and Jockey' we had questions fired at us on all sides as we seemed to arouse great interest. Before we left, Herbert took a picture of the (self-styled) scruffiest landlord in the country, whose inn was the only one not to serve chips.

Our haven of rest tonight is Virginia Cottage at Stone-aston. Another 17th century building. When we arrived we were greeted by a venerable gentleman who showed us to our room (comfortable and clean) and this time with a telly, so presumably we are expected to disappear after the meal which, thank goodness, we are having in tonight. Our host, who we see from a steel trunk outside our room was a major in the regular army, told us he had been a bursar at Ampleforth when Archbishop Hume was the principal. His wife, Irene, came in eventually. She is much younger. Major Watson had already told us his first wife had died of cancer. Now we are bathed (once more), changed and awaiting our dinner. Herbert has just told me we have walked 230 miles – our longest stint ever.

8.45 pm. This is becoming 'a good food guide to walkers'. Major Watson's wife 'just loves' cooking. We were given prawn cocktail, with dainty squares of brown bread and butter, chicken en croute, lots of fresh vegetables and new potatoes, and strawberry cream sponge – all homemade. Quite magnificent. Afterwards Irene came and talked to us while mine host watched the telly which had been on non-stop since we arrived. They provided a contrast. He is the epitome of a cultured English gentleman – elegant, dignified, ex-army. She is a friendly ex-cook, quite plump, curly hair, old T-shirt, jeans, trainers. We liked them both very much indeed. Irene runs the village bingo club. He seems to spend his time gardening (and watching TV). Another happy overnight stay.

Day 22 – 9th May – Thursday Sunny.

Fresh orange juice for breakfast. Fascinating little house. Original 17th century stone spiral staircase rising from the dining room; very old oak beam over the ancient fireplace; a bit untidy, but a relaxing atmosphere; old beams in bedroom ceiling; ornate banister with a decorated centrepiece in ceiling; wooden doors with wrought iron latches; old stone walls in corridors.

4.30 pm. Bath. Kinlet Guest House. The first part of our walk today has been on minor roads or footpaths across fields where – what a thrill! – we saw a deer which raced away from us as fast as it could. The sunlit countryside is magical, and we went through a number of quiet little villages until we reached the A367, then on to an old Roman road, the Fosseway. This went up steeply but was pleasanter than the busy road. Sadly this lovely lane returned to the A367 and we had to continue on this until reaching our B & B (99 Wellsway). Our landlady was out so we went in search of tea and are now sitting in 'The Bear' enjoying tea and cakes, particularly welcome as we've had no lunch today. At lunchtime we had deviated to find a pub which appeared on the map, but on reaching it found it to be closed. The next – up a steep hill – only produced cider. Apart from the barmaid there was only one other person there – an elderly local. We had a friendly time with them, and the girl behind the bar offered us some 'rough' cider to try. Well, we are in the West Country where the cider apples are grown, so why not? I was given only a sip. Too much and you are flat on the floor.

9.00 pm. Ready for bed. This is an unprepossessing terraced house, with Corinthian decoration, but is in fact Victorian. Inside it is spacious, airy, very comfortable, and we are quite happy to spend two nights here. We have a big sunny room with a window seat. Very good bed. There was a lot of mail from Jane, plus maps. Letters from Lesley, Peggie, Gordon, a card from all the local preachers and many of Herbert's friends. Very touching to read all their good wishes. Jane is marvellous.

We went back to 'The Bear' for a meal (not up to Irene's

standard), then had a long talk with our hostess. She is very interested in our walk and wants to contribute. We are still going well, but looking forward to a day's rest tomorrow. Hope to have a bus tour of Bath. Today we left Somerset and are now in the County of Avon. We loved the softness and tranquillity of Somerset with its thatched cottages in peaceful villages; wonderful English landscape. Now we have the Cotswolds to look forward to.

Day off – 10th May – Friday Dry, bright.

We've had a very long night. We awakened eventually at ten past nine. Two snags in an otherwise good B & B. 1. Traffic – which roars past continually. 2. Shortage of loos. There's only one for all visitors and that is in with the bath and shower. Jenny, our landlady, said if we're stuck we can use hers. So in the early hours (6.15 am to be precise) we went downstairs, through the kitchen (don't let the cat out), through the laundry room, take door on left. By request we've had no cooked breakfast, but brown toast, fruit yoghurt, muesli, orange juice. Would you believe, our hostess has got us complimentary tickets for the (quite expensive) bus tour of the city? She is going to DRIVE us to the station where we pick it up. What fun!

2.15 pm. The bus tour lasted an hour but we can use the ticket all day if we wish. We were on an open-top bus and were shown the whole city. The famous Circus, the Royal Crescent, the Abbey, glorious gardens and many terraces of 18th century Palladian houses. Then we were taken up the hills that overlook Bath, and the whole panorama over the city and beyond was a magnificent sight. A conducted tour of the Roman baths was the next excitement. Much has been excavated in the last hundred years, but the mineral spring which the Romans discovered was again used by fashionable people in the 18th century, mainly because Queen Anne believed the waters would cure her of her many ailments. Thus started the history of fashionable Bath. The aristocracy flocked here to taste the waters and to parade up and down the broad pavements in their elegant clothes. The Royal

Crescent was originally built as lodging houses for wealthy Londoners. We were shown the house where Jane Austen lived, and where she wrote her satire on contemporary life in Bath, 'Northanger Abbey'.

Weary after our tour of the museum we are now in the famous Sally Lunn coffee shop which is the oldest house in Bath. Its bow-fronted window of an earlier period overlooks another crescent of classical buildings and an elegant stone courtyard where no cars are allowed. We've both had a huge Sally Lunn bun topped with smoked salmon paté and the best cup of tea since we left home. After this excellent lunch we paid 25p for a deckchair in the flower-filled park in the centre of Bath. A visit to Bath Abbey and another bus tour completed our 'day off' and we returned, by taxi, to our digs.

After another meal at 'The Bear' we spoke to Jane who is staying with Peter, en route for Hungary. Our hostess has gone out, putting up a 'no vacancies' sign so we are on our own tonight which has its advantages. Tomorrow we will be on the road again. Jennie Bennett – the proprietor of the Kinlet Guest House, is a gentle, cultured lady, widow of a research doctor, and has lived 13 years in the US. Both children are still there. She is very attached to her mother (78) who is at present in hospital with a damaged back. Jenny is very worried about her. She thinks she'll give up the guest house and go and live with her. There are so many human joys and sorrows when you meet people on your travels. Jennie has taken a sponsor form and has already raised £25 for CA.

Day 23 – 11th May – Saturday

We bade farewell to Jennie who would only charge us for one night, and started on the Cotswold Way. This begins officially at the Pump Room, which is an elegant, 18th century establishment with glass chandeliers, decorated ceiling, a quartet playing appropriate music, and with catering by Mr Michael Milburn, formerly of Sunderland. We left a message for Michael who, we were informed by a gentleman in a dinner jacket, was 'on vacation in France'.

Our walk took us past the Royal Crescent and through Queen Victoria's Park, so named by the residents who tried to make amends for an unfortunate remark about the monarch's fat legs which she overheard. Then it was uphill all the morning until we reached the escarpment with panoramic views of the surrounding countryside. We could see the city for a very long time, but it eventually faded into the distance so that we felt at last we were making progress. As we are now on an official footpath there are quite a few hikers about. Apart from the lovely landscape, an added bonus is the fact that it is very well signposted. To our dismay we had another very steep climb before reaching our destination – Cold Ashton. And what surprises were in store for us there! We had been told by our landlady exactly where her house was, but we could hardly believe we had found the right one. It is a perfect gem of a country house, just beside the church, with an immaculate garden. Inside it is so exotic that we really feel out of our element. The bedroom is so beautifully decorated and furnished that I took a picture of it. The bathroom would put the Hilton to shame – although for the first time we have no washbasin in our bedroom. The other snag is – no evening meal, so before long we have to put our weary feet back into their boots and set off in search of food.

9.00 pm. A good meal, followed by an interesting conversation with two Cotswold Way walkers who wanted to record what we said. We'll probably meet this couple again during the next week.

Today we were free of the danger of fast cars, but on passing a golf course we were warned of the dangers from flying golfballs. The hazards of long distance walking!

We have been appalled by the rigorous conditions imposed on the poor B & Bs by the authoritarian tourist boards. The people running them are all obliged to take a course on 'food hygiene' for which they must pay £15 and spend all day having lessons in this mysterious art, and for this they receive a certificate to hang up for their guests to see. Jennie, of Bath, told us she is inspected regularly. One day one of these inspectors found her cat on the table drinking the milk from a jug. One of her friends was in deep trouble because a hygiene expert had found her shopping basket on the kitchen table. The basket might have been put on a shop floor which could have germs on it.

Day 24 – 12th May – Sunday Cold Ashton.

It is appropriately named. The reception yesterday by our hostess was chilly in that, on arrival we were immediately rushed upstairs, with the words 'This is your bedroom, this is the bathroom and this is your sitting room' (a tiny alcove taken off the landing with three uncomfortable chairs, a table and a TV) and we realised she didn't wish to see us again until breakfast time. This we have just finished in the conservatory overlooking the immaculately landscaped and entirely weedless garden. The conservatory is the last word in luxury, as is the entire house – or as much of it as we were allowed to see. The ornate bedroom with its thick pile carpet, matching bedcovers and wallpaper, valuable china ornaments and dainty dried flower arrangements, made our own home seem very humble in comparison. The parish church, just the other side of the garden, has no service today (only 1st and 3rd Sundays) but we are 'free to look around it'. So we'll do that, then set off on the next leg of our pilgrimage.

12.45 pm. Church was locked up. Today the Cotswold Way has led us through fields, woods and villages of old stone houses, and we have just emerged from a forest path into a clearing with picnic tables and chairs, and even better – toilets! So we are now eating our little Melton Mowbray pies, which we had the foresight to purchase at a garage in Cold Ashton before leaving. The sun has come out and beside us are a group of very jolly Dutch people who have come over on the ferry for the weekend. Also a Welsh family en route from Brighton to S. Wales. Grandpa who was with them was so Welsh he was unintelligible. Then we were on our way again. The excellent signposting failed us at one point and we were in danger of trespassing on land belonging to a very stately 'stately home'. We retraced our steps when we were confronted with a terse 'Private, keep out', but not before a pony and trap approached us with two men aboard. As soon as we retreated the vehicle turned round and disappeared. (They must have had telescopes fixed on us).

We had another obstacle to overcome this morning, as the Cotswold Way, like our experiences in Devon, was blocked by an electric fence. Took a picture of Herbert very cautiously crawling underneath.

We were quite tired this afternoon, but by 3.45 pm we'd reached our next haven, The Dornden Guest House. This is a big Georgian house in large grounds (there is a ha-ha in true Jane Austen style in the lawn) and we have a sunny bedroom overlooking the garden. So far it isn't as welcoming as some of the smaller guest houses we've been in, but we reserve judgement.

Later. No marks for this one! The meal was both expensive and poor. Another one to wipe the dust from off our feet. The only other diner was a maiden lady who, silent at first, soon began talking at a great rate. Had a 23-year-old Morris Minor. Lived in Dorset. Had just become a pensioner and thought of starting a B & B as her pension wasn't 'quite enough'. I hope it will be better than this one.

Day 25 – 13th May – Monday Foggy.

Breakfast. Here are our Dutch friends again. The little maiden lady was still excessively talkative, probably lonely but also very kind. She will ring our B & B tonight with an address in Stratford.

12.25 pm. Hillesley. 'The Fleece'. Lunch. We keep meeting four Canadian hikers. Very good fun. Bob Robinson (ex Yorkshire) now Canadian. Gave us his card. Owns 'The Wellington Restaurant' on Lake Ontario. (Why hike in England? we asked. Appalachian trail – mosquitos in north, snakes in south. Rockies – must have a guide, too cold in winter, too hot in summer, no B & Bs. They prefer England.)

Helicopters and postmen. At Horton, which we walked through today, we enquired from a friendly postman where the post office was. He waved his hands to indicate it was no more. So we set off down the hill, but he overtook us in his van and stopped and told us why. He had been on the same route for 40 years. The villages round here are dying, he said. There's no shop, no post office, no pub, no school, no church and no people. The village houses have been bought by outsiders and turned into 'mini-palaces' with two cars. (We passed quite a few of these, some of them converted barns.) The people were all out working, we were told. No village community life was possible. This sad tale reminded us of the story about Cold Ashton, where the old parish church was closed two Sundays in the month and the large Elizabethan mansion there is owned by the son of Sir Robert McAlpine, who arrives and leaves by helicopter.

Map reading. Only a blind halfwit could lose his way on the Cotswold Way, which boasts that it is the best directed path in the country. We have lost it twice. This morning the arrow pointed somewhere towards the pole star which left us confused. Eileen said, 'We should go towards that tree on the horizon and see where it goes.' Herbert said, 'We should go north.' So we went north, to the left, round a field which would eventually have taken us back to the place where we started. It wasn't long before Herbert sensed he had made a terrible mistake. So we went back to the tree on the horizon, and there was the road we were looking for and the next arrow. Female intuition, not the compass won that round.

We cheated today. The Cotswold Way was such a meander, and uphill to boot, that most of the time we have stuck to the road. It has been a very pleasant walk nevertheless. The countryside is full of colour and as the sun came out after lunch it looked even more lovely. Very hilly, tree covered country, with huge flowering chestnuts in red and white, cow parsley decorating the hedges like delicate white lace. As we neared North Nibley, our destination for tonight, a huge monument appeared high up on a hill. This was a memorial to William Tyndale who was born near here. Earlier we'd seen, and photographed, another monument. This one was called 'The Somerset Monument'. Why? We are not even in Somerset.

North Nibley – 6.00 pm. Our guest house tonight is in

complete contrast to last night's – and we know that life is made up of contrasts. Cold Ashton was unfriendly, expensive and altogether poor value for money. This evening we have been warmly welcomed by an elderly gentleman who made us tea as soon as we arrived, and sat beside us in the rather shabby sitting room chatting to us while we drank it. More and more we are made to realise that it is people who matter, not places. This is an old house, with none of the luxury we have found in some of our habitats which were like the postman's 'mini palaces'. It is clean, and we are going to be fed. Hurrah!

Later – a homely meal, and a very sweet couple. They are trying to sell their house. For many years the little shop across the road belonged to them, but they felt they were too old to keep it going. After a sociable evening spent in the company of our host and hostess and the only other guest, a young man who was doing his first long distance walk (he had blisters), I said goodnight, but mine host insisted on taking me up to the attic to show me loads of old photographs, mostly of his marriage, which was very touching. The young man has warned us off the accommodation we had thought of for tomorrow – soft bed, noisy. No thank you. At 2.00 pm today we reached Alderly – the boundary of Avon – and are now in Gloucestershire. We're making progress.

Day 26 – 14th May – Tuesday

It was raining last night, but is now fine and sunny (9.00 am). This little B & B at North Nibley continues to surprise and please us. We have had a hearty breakfast, and now Herbert is busy telling Geordie stories to the son-in-law of our hostess (a very appreciative audience) so I don't know when we'll get away.

2.00 pm. Somewhere on the Cotswold Way. We've had a *very* hard morning's climbing. Magnificent views over the escarpment, but we'll never reach John o' Groats by following the official footpath (same story as in Cornwall). We did some shopping in Durseley, an attractive market town approached by a steep drop among huge beech trees which formed a delicate green lace canopy overhead. Many important-looking houses occupied large areas of ground. We are now in wealthy Gloucestershire. We had a satisfactory encounter with a walker going in the opposite direction who was suitably impressed when we told him our ultimate destination (which he asked). This made us forget our aching limbs, tired feet and hunger, for a while at least – until we started the relentless climb again.

6.30 pm. The Kings Head, Kings Stanley. After lunch yesterday – along the road with cars whizzing by – we journeyed on 'The Way' until at last we had our reward. We were 778 ft above sea level. It was a clear day and the view over the Severn Valley to the Welsh hills beyond was breathtaking. An AA plaque pointed out all the places we could see, including the Black Mountains 40 miles away. After 'drinking deep' of all this beauty we went, rather reluctantly, back to the Cotswold Way path which seems determined to tire us out. It led us right round the escarpment above which gliders were floating. We were walking all the while through the most beautiful beech trees adorned in their light spring colours. About 4.30 pm we descended steeply to the little town of Kings Stanley where we are spending the night. Our young friend of yesterday having successfully warned us off the only B & B, a converted chapel, we have opted for this inn which is very comfortable. So now, bathed and gradually recovering, we are awaiting the magic hour of 7 o'clock when we can eat.

9.00 pm. It was a *terrible* meal. But – another surprise awaited us. The only other couple in an otherwise empty bar lounge (the food perhaps?) said to me (Herbert was on the phone to Helen), 'Are you the people who have walked from Penzance?' 'No, Lands End.' Apparently they had met the man who had been so impressed yesterday. We had a very happy evening with these two young people, and before we left to go to bed the husband took out his cheque book and to our surprise, and also his wife's, wrote out a cheque for £50 for CA.

Rob is home from Australia and they are all going to meet

us in Broadway on Saturday. The other item of excitement is that the TV people are desperate to meet us. Evidently they contacted Peggie, who put them on to Carr House; Gillian told them to ring Helen who said she had no idea where we were. They left a phone number which Helen gave us, and Herbert has telephoned to tell them where we will be tomorrow. So we'll see what happens. This is Christian Aid week and there is so much pressure on the organisation because of the many world disasters, they want us to have as much publicity as possible – even us!

Day 27 – 15th May – Wednesday Fine, chilly, good walking weather.

Breakfast of brown bread, cereal and fruit. Chatted to two-year-old Jessica, landlord's daughter. Also chatted to the landlord about his tank of exotic marine fish – an all-absorbing hobby apparently. This couple took the pub over, a year ago when it was very run down and they are gradually renovating it. We had the whole of the top floor to ourselves which was very peaceful; but they do need to do something about the food.

11.35 am. Edgemoor Inn (just outside Painswick). A splendid morning's walk with panoramic views all around us. A herd of galloping heifers raced towards us at one point but Herbert was too scared to photograph them. We were told later that they are harmless, just curious. We walked through

The Curious Heifers

more beech woods, this time full of bluebells. In view of the distance yet to cover we bypassed one more Cotswold deviation. There's no doubt 'The Way' is always the most scenic, but we must keep our eye on the ball.

4.25 pm. In bed, bathed and drinking tea – this is the life. Although the guide book assures us we have walked 10 miles, we find it hard to believe. After lunch we walked first downhill then up again into a gem of a Cotswold village – Painswick. All the buildings are in the soft grey Cotswold stone, all in the same style of architecture, high gabled roofs and dormer windows, very tall chimneys. Nothing jars. Our place of rest this evening is one of the most attractive so far. The house is in the centre of the village, next to the parish church. The churchyard is full of large, carefully shaped, but very dark and forbidding yew trees which we are told are over 400 years old. Downstairs is a teashop – where we are going to eat tonight (no going out, thank goodness). Our room is furnished in pinewood, there is an old Cotswold stone fireplace, and stone mullions at the windows. When we arrived at the teashop we saw the young couple who had donated £50 last night (Mr & Mrs Swallow). They were having lunch and were then going to walk another 7 miles. We told them we were having a half day.

After booking in we went for a short wander round the village. The post office, which was closed, is a 15th century building, half timbered with an ancient wooden door. It is so famous they sell postcards of it. Then we went to an equally old and attractive building owned by the National Trust where visitors can buy secondhand books. We bought a Jane Austen but not the one about Bath unfortunately. Herbert took some photographs and we have now retired for the rest of the day. British Telecom are tearing up all the streets and making a dreadful noise which is sacrilege in this lovely place. This appears to be a B & B which concentrates on food, not drink like the pub last night, so we'll probably have something better to eat tonight.

The telly man has just telephoned. We are meeting him and his crew at 11.00 am tomorrow.

9.00 pm. A cordon bleu meal tonight, cooked exquisitely

by the husband and served by the wife. After we had finished they both sat and talked to us. They work very hard. As well as running a B & B, their restaurant serves morning coffee, lunch, afternoon tea and, booked in advance, dinner. They'd like to retire to Devon, near the sea.

Day 28 – 16th May – Thursday Our TV debut. Dull, cold.

We bade a fond farewell to our hosts, Mr & Mrs Mansfield. We had a long chat with them at breakfast. They were very disillusioned with the young people of Painswick. 'It's the worst village in England for girls getting pregnant – they breed like rabbits.' It did occur to us that there really wasn't much in the way of entertainment here. There was a notice directing us to some Rococo gardens (which unfortunately we had no time to visit) but perhaps these were not particularly appealing to teenagers.

We arrived at our assignation point with the TV crew half an hour early, having walked through more of the enchanting Cotswold beechwoods. As we were walking towards an inn to fill in the time drinking coffee, a pretty young girl approached us – 'Mr & Mrs Witherington?' she enquired. Isn't it marvellous to be recognised out in the wilds! She was the first of the team to arrive and she gave us coffee and biscuits – very acceptable as it was so cold. Then another car arrived, then another until there were five in all. The entertainment began. First we all walked up to the desired location – a romantic spot among the trees overlooking the escarpment. After that things became a bit confused. The director issued a number of instructions but the cameraman said he had a problem. Their hired equipment wasn't functioning as it should. Herbert and I decided to retire to a nearby log to rest our feet while this was sorted out. Finally we were summoned and our bit began. The presenter – a pleasant young man called Tom – had already made his introduction which we hadn't heard, and we were then invited to walk along the path with him while he asked us questions. This, for some technical reason, was sound only. Then it was vision only as Tom joined us on our walk. We were told not to look surprised to see him. We weren't. As this time it was vision only it didn't matter what we said. The next stage was to photograph our boots, first walking towards the camera, then away from it. They will send us a video of both the edited and unedited versions. We said goodbye to them and continued on our way, and it was only later we realised, with disappointment, that we hadn't taken a photograph of them.

It's been a long day. This morning we walked up and down the Cotswold Way on a narrow path surrounded on both sides by trees, so there was no view, which is always tedious. About 2.00 pm we arrived in Birdslip and had to go to a very large and expensive hotel for a sandwich as there was nothing else open. Again we reluctantly abandoned 'The Way' which went off in its convoluted fashion, continually doubling the distance, and we walked to Cheltenham along the B4070. Until about 5.00 pm there was a complete lack of B & Bs but eventually we found one. A friendly man opened the door. Yes, he had a room, but no, no meal. However, he kindly telephoned to a friend who would give us both – and, what is more, was willing to come in his car to pick us up. As it was by now raining heavily we were more than grateful. So here we are, at Hallery House, run by Steve and Angie. We are glad to stop.

To return to our brief sojourn at lunchtime, perhaps two untidy hikers weren't all that welcome at The George, Birdslip. I thought that in view of the expensive interior I'd better at least comb my hair. So I went to the 'ladies' and started rummaging in my haversack for my comb which obstinately refused to appear. There wasn't much room for manoeuvre and two elegant ladies were obviously getting impatient. 'Perhaps I'd better get out of your way,' I said (very politely). '*If* you wouldn't mind,' was the equally polite reply. So I did that.

Our B & B tonight is rather disappointing after our teashop in Painswick, although more expensive (but we are in Cheltenham after all). The building has a rather fine classical façade with an elegant entrance hall, but the visitor is obliged to walk past two glass fish tanks, one of which contains two black and vicious-looking fish, the other, two equally horrid crabs. Inside, it is a bit shabby and the original garden has been sold off as building lots and there are a number of small modern villas just beneath our window. But if we look over these there is a view of the Cotswold hills which on a fine day must be worth seeing. Today it is foggy, so we'll go and try their food. The young proprietor kindly brought us some tea, also a blackboard with the menu written on it. There is a telly, and we were much encouraged to learn from the local news that we are now in the Midlands, so we are really making great strides. PS. Our TV fee is going to CA.

Day 29 – 17th May – Friday Raining!

But we were very lucky at the beginning and I expect the sun will come back one day. An interesting breakfast. Home-made rolls, cheese, strawberries. But Herbert's porridge was no better than the meat last night (which was awful). And our hostess is so very proud of 'my chef'. Steve and Angie contributed £10 in spite of their obvious financial difficulties. All the B & Bs say how slow business is. Today we have walked right through Cheltenham, parts of which are as impressive as Bath and parts which are just like any other modern, uninteresting, crowded and litter-filled town. Then it was uphill all the way until we were 1,000 ft above sea level – our highest point yet. We ate our picnic looking back towards Cheltenham which we could see far down in the valley below us. We crossed 'The Gallop' – a large flat area used for training racehorses, then on to the Cotswold Way again, across fields, rejoining the road to Winchcombe where we are staying tonight. We are both very tired, but we always recover after a bath and a meal. Our B & B is locked up so we are sitting drinking tea in the Lady Jayne Teashop next door.

Some funny notices 1. No parking at all times
2. Footpath and style (*sic.*)

We passed an ancient burial ground today. 2,000 BC. Belas Knap. 28 skeletons were discovered 100 years ago.

6.00 pm. We are now installed in 'Mercia'. This is an

ancient Cotswold cottage, complete with oak beams and sloping walls and floors. We've had a bath and are gathering strength to go out to eat. Herbert is having trouble with his toe joints which have been painful today. But I've massaged them well, and we are hoping a night's sleep will put matters right.

Day 30 – 18th May – Saturday

It looks as if the sun will break through after many dull days. We've both slept well – and I had no dreams for the first time since we began. This house is 500 years old. We had a pretty bedroom, and as no other guests were staying, a bathroom, loo and sitting room with TV all to ourselves. Jean Upton and husband Trevor (solicitor?) are Methodists. Jean was preparing for a coffee morning (for the Kurds) so Methodism in the Cotswolds is the same as Methodism everywhere else. A lovely breakfast. Nothing plastic. Brown granary bread, fruit, fresh grapefruit. Lace cloth, dainty china – just our sort of place. We'd love to stay on for a few days but on we go. We meet Helen and family at 3.00 pm.

2.00 pm. We had a good morning's walk. All our troubles of yesterday have gone – the rain, tiredness, Herbert's foot troubles – and we've been walking on air. True – we cut out a big hill on 'The Way', so have not had any climbing to do. We've been through some beautiful Cotswold villages. They seem completely untouched by time (that is if you discount the television aerials). One in particular was quite enchanting. The traditional high gabled buildings in golden stone surrounded an apple orchard with enormous purple irises growing along the roadside. We walked through the parkland of an aristocratic home with an elegant lodge gate, private chapel, flowering trees everywhere. We wanted to photograph everything.

People. We met four 14-year-olds doing the Duke of Edinburgh Award. They had to carry one quarter of their body weight – a stone and a half. Only for one day and a night, but really! We met an uppercrust gent who was suitably amazed when he was given the answer to 'where have you come from – going to?' Another posh guy with three large dogs who'd lost his pedometer. We took his address and said we'd send it to him if we found it – we didn't. We met a middle-aged Welsh couple (wife very pretty) who talked for ages. They were in a caravan somewhere.

Now we have been refreshed with our usual sandwiches, cider and coffee and are ready to meet the family. Our host last night contributed £2 to CA. He was very talkative. Had recently had extensive repairs to the ancient house – a damp proof course had been put in and the builders had uncovered the original daub and wattle walls, also a 500-year-old oak beam which was in perfect condition. The work cost £250 per day. Trevor had wanted the old beams exposed but that would have meant another four days' work. He would need a lot of B & B clients to cover that. At the White Hart last night we had a very good meal (chicken cordon bleu very nicely done). We avoided John Wesley House as it was expensive, but were amused to see the sign 'John Wesley House – fully licensed'. What would he have said? It must make him turn in his grave.

Day 31 – 19th May – Sunday Weather improving.

Overnight at Henly in Arden at a dreadful Victorian B & B. Helen had tried 25 before getting fixed up, so it was disappointing for her. Never mind – it was lovely to be with the Hallidays. They met us as we were walking along an unclassified road near the unspoilt village of Stanton. Sandwiches at The Mountain Inn (aptly named as it was at the top of a steep hill). We all piled into the Rover and we directed Rob back to see some of the small villages which had so enchanted us, then there was quite a long drive, through Broadway and Stratford to our overnight stop. This house is completely cluttered with Victorian memorabilia, in particular dozens of ancient china dolls. There are dolls everywhere – in cots, high chairs, glass cases, all staring at us with their glassy eyes in an uncanny way. A musty smell hung over everything and we thought with nostalgia of our lovely place at Winchcombe the previous night. The proprietor, a coloured gentleman of uncertain origin, was continually reprimanding Michael and Christopher, who with their usual boisterous cheerfulness threatened the peace and quiet of this mausoleum. No evening meal was on offer so we went (by car) to the nearest pub and had a very poor bar meal, paid for by Rob. Then back to sit in the ghastly lounge (although it was nice and warm) to see lots of Halliday photos – many of the great reunion at Whitburn on New Year's Eve.

Rob drove us back to our point of meeting, and after a long photographic session we said goodbye. It has really been kind of them to make the effort to come and see us. It was a long way, a big expense, and had to be fitted in between Michael's tennis lesson yesterday and his football match today.

1.00 pm. We are in a little coffee shop in Broadway having a sandwich. It's been another enjoyable walk over the fields covered in buttercups, and with an enchanting view over the Vale of Gloucester. We are now in the county of Warwick – another county behind us. We have been through yet more of the tiny, almost unreal Cotswold villages – high gabled, flower-covered houses in golden stone; the wisteria and clematis in profusion everywhere; immaculate lawns, rhododendron, azalea, lilac, flowering chestnut always before our eyes. I persuaded Herbert to photograph some dainty deep-blue wild flowers (name unknown) covering a steep bank beside the road.

We met a couple who directed us when we were unsure of the way. They live in Solihull and to our amazement told us we are now only 28 miles from Birmingham.

3.10 pm. Chipping Campden reached. The end of the Cotswold Way (102 miles). Beginning of the Heart of England Way. This is another picture postcard village. Sitting on a seat in the centre we are looking at a long street of 'olde worlde' Cotswold stone houses, the old steeply gabled roofs all of different levels, tiny windows with leaded panes, the whole picture completely spoiled by all the cars, both parked and squeezing their way along the narrow street. It's Sunday, but, as in Broadway, all the shops and cafes are open and doing a roaring trade. It has been a very pleasant and, after the steep climb out of Broadway, a very easy high level walk in the meadows among the cows and young calves, and with great vistas all around on which to feast our eyes. Another three miles, then we will look for a 'nice' B & B.

5.20 pm. Yes – we have found one at Mickleton. Much cheaper than yesterday and much better. En suite, TV, friendly welcome. The Heart of England is an improvement on the Cotswold Way so far. It is pleasant and easy and well signposted. We were even allowed diagonally across fields which were full of crops. Again we were high up with panoramic views. We met four hikers who had just finished the Cotswold Way (in less time than we had taken). They agreed with us that the cheapest B & Bs are the best. Flash-back to the postman at Horton and the dead villages – these walkers had been talking to a binman who said that in many of the villages you could learn a lot by what people put in their dustbins, such as grass cuttings and bottles. They don't even eat in their houses. They go to restaurants, come home, cut the grass, have a glass of wine, go to bed then off to work in the morning.

Chipping Camden

8.30 pm. Just in from The Kings Head. An excellent meal of home cooked ham, salad and homemade rolls. Herbert, rice pud. Me, a gorgeous lemon sorbet. We are going to watch our serial (Tinker Tailor) then go to bed. For the *first* time we are not exhausted. We must be over the hump.

Mickleton, unlike the more picturesque villages we've been through, is alive and well. Our landlady told us there is a good mix of generations and types of housing. There are two shops, a post office and a school. In the old inn last night there was *no* fruit machine and the clientele seemed to be local, not visitors. The stone mushrooms we see everywhere were originally designed to sit under the wooden barns to keep the hay dry and free of rats. We saw some in situ underneath a cricket pavilion in Stanton.

* * *

The Great British Institution

One curious friend enquired, what did we talk about for three months? We had to think about that one, but the answer wasn't long in coming. We talked about B & Bs; in the mornings about the one we had just left, and in the afternoons about the one we were going to – or hoping we were going to. That is an over-simplification, of course, but anyone reading the diary will realise how big a part our nightly accommodation played in the general experiences of each day. Perhaps there should have been much more about the scenery, wild life, architecture and so on, but this is not a gazeteer; it is the story of getting from A to B on each individual day. So, what concerns you most are of course the weather, the gradients, the state of the footpaths or the traffic on the roads, but supremely what is at A and what is at B. From our very varied experiences on previous long distance walks, we have come to realise that a walk is remembered not so much for the magnificence of the terrain or even the weather; it is remembered for the places where we stayed, and we can still recount what happened when we arrived at Bilsdale in 1980, or the quality of the lamb chops at

Ravenstonedale or Peter Bunny's stone staircase at Broughton.

After sleeping in 93 different beds – no, that is not correct because we stayed five nights with Jane at the beginning of the Pennine Way – we ended up with a vast store of experience covering every single detail of the services provided; for instance, whether the butter is in those horrid bits of tin foil which make such a mess of your fingers when you try to unwrap them, and if so, how many are you given. We knew it all. On previous walks we used to award marks out of 10 for each place, but on this marathon we became so bogged down with detail that it would have been necessary to use a computer and award marks out of several thousand. This of course is the fascination of staying at B & Bs. If you are staying at Hiltons or Travelodges or Post Houses you know exactly what to expect and in a very short space of time it becomes one great bore. But B & Bs are of an infinite variety; no two are the same, and each night there are those special surprises which you never expected, such as the colour of the loo seat or the extra tea bags provided in case the tea isn't strong enough.

So first and foremost, we say thank you to those kind ladies and gentlemen who welcomed us into their homes, despite the slightly wild and unkempt appearance which we must have presented on their doorstep. Whilst we would sometimes wonder what we had let ourselves in for when the door opened, we have no doubt whatsoever that the poor soul on the other side would wonder what he or she had let themselves in for. By the time we were bathed and changed we managed to give a more reassuring impression, but on arrival we were never a pretty sight. It must be a remarkable act of faith to let unknown creatures take over part of your house, and in two minutes cover your lovingly tidied room with the unimaginable contents of their rucksacks, and spread wet, muddy garments around as though it were the local rugby club changing rooms. But they did so cheerfully and without complaint, and we thank them sincerely.

It is no use trying to lay down guidelines in advance of

course; you take what comes along and are thankful. The bottom line of our requirements was that the establishment should be clean, and with just one or two notable exceptions, they all were clean. Anything else was a bonus, and there were a lot of bonuses. We slept in beautiful beds and bathed in beautiful baths, and at times dined in beautiful dining rooms. We tried desperately hard to persuade our hosts and hostesses to provide us with an evening meal, perhaps at times too hard, for the simple reason that once you stop it is very difficult to start up again. Understandably several were reluctant to slave in the kitchen for a couple of strangers, and pointed us to a nearby pub or restaurant. This was really the only inducement to stay in a hotel where you were more or less guaranteed an evening meal; but the more we stayed in hotels, the more we were convinced that B & Bs were preferable. Occasionally we would come across that category of reception which said, 'There's your room; there's the bath; the pub is round the corner; see you at breakfast,' but generally of course B & Bs are intensely personal: in the majority you not only borrow a bedroom, but you share a home, which is their great charm and interest. And really this book should be dedicated to that long, long list of dear people who greeted us as strangers and bade farewell as friends.

We never had much energy left for the evenings. If we arrived early after a short day we would often go to bed and sleep for a couple of hours before the evening meal. We carried one or two permissible excess weights for recreation only. We had a travelling Scrabble (though seldom had the strength to play it) and a paperback – once it was half a paperback as we cut it in two so one could read the beginning and the other the end. We also took the smallest New Testament we could find, but the print was so tiny we could hardly read it. So our evenings were not notable for their activity: it was a question of recovering from the day's labours and preparing for the next, massaging away the aches and pains (which were mainly psychological anyway) and resting the weary limbs. There is no doubt that, as grandparents, you have to pace yourselves, otherwise there is the danger of suffering from the effects of cumulative exhaustion. We were introduced to that in the Himalayas and its principle symptom is the conviction that you cannot possibly walk another step, so – as they say in Geordieland – ga' canny.

*   *   *

Day 32 – 20th May – Monday Bright, sunny morning.

The weather report last night forecast 70°. We go to Stratford today. Driving through it in Rob's car yesterday we were not impressed.

1.00 pm. Lunch in a field of new mown hay. The sun is shining and we are at peace with the world. At breakfast we met an elderly couple (like us) with a mother of 97. They were from West Hartlepool and were visiting their daughter who had become disillusioned with modern life and was living communally in a weird sort of meditative order. They went to great lengths to assure us it was not religious. It is an international setup and people go to it to 'find themselves'. This girl (now 40) had been married and divorced and had at last found happiness with these people. I asked the parents if they would like to join it, but they said very definitely NO!

We left Mickleton at our usual hour (10.00 am). Our hostess contributed £1. We soon found The Heart of England Way with its excellent directions – mostly across fields, although one farmer ignored the 'Way's' instructions and directed us round the edge. Then, quite unaccountably, we lost it. This was not a disaster as we had intended leaving it to visit Stratford. Sadly *Henry IV* Pt. 1 isn't on while we are here.

5.15 pm. Stratford. An idyllic afternoon's walk through sunlit meadows. A beautiful summer day, with the scent of lilac and may blossom in every village. We passed through the grounds of Alscot Park – a stately home, probably 18th century. Battlements, stone balustrades, deer park. I think we were trespassing as we came across the public footpath later. We passed through Preston-on-Stour – another picturebook village with village green, an old timbered manor house and a majestic parish church.

Architecture. Red brick, very mellow. Windows with elaborately patterned leaded panes, all painted white.

We walked along the river into Stratford, then crossed it on a ferry – worked by a young girl smoking a cigarette. She had to turn a handle which moved the ferry boat along a chain. We had a look at the Royal Shakespeare Theatre, which is enormous, and built in the local red brick, but there's nothing on we want to see. We booked in at a very basic B & B (East Bank House, large Victorian building) and will have to go out to eat unfortunately.

The things people say – Lady in Tourist Board on hearing the length of our journey – 'Do you do this often?'

We have had a meal at a posh restaurant (The Cellar, which really was a cellar in Victorian times). It had a vaulted brick ceiling. We returned to our 'digs' and rang Jane who we thought would be back from Hungary. She and Keith were at the theatre so spoke to Gillian. Forecast for tomorrow – hotter than today – help! Herbert is disappointed we still get tired after 10 miles. Perhaps the heat was the trouble today. It's really weather for sitting in deckchairs.

The Theatre, Stratford

Day 33 – 21st May – Tuesday Fine and Sunny.

We had rather a disturbed night. It was very hot and there was a lot of noisy traffic. When it started up again early this morning we decided to get up. It's going to be another hot day. We'll go back briefly to Stratford for a few necessary items (like money) then off towards Birmingham. 'The Heart' goes between Birmingham and Coventry.

5.15 pm. Claverdon. This has been a day of surprises. We left Stratford by the main road and after about 1½ miles walked along a pretty minor road until we reached the village of Slitterfield. Thirsty as usual we were about to investigate one of the two pubs when, lo and behold, there, right in the centre of the village was the Methodist Church, and surprise, surprise, there was a coffee morning on. Even more surprising the name of the minister on the noticeboard was that of one of Herbert's old friends. We walked in, two hot, untidy hikers, to confront the usual Methodist gathering of old ladies and one young man who was the minister. We were very kindly received, given orange squash and coffee, and Derek Morton – the minister – was delighted to see Herbert.

We haven't made a lot of progress today. After our coffee break we walked quite a way uphill and at 12.30 were so hot and sticky that we found a grassy place by the roadside where we had our Stratford M & S sandwiches and promptly fell asleep. Rousing ourselves reluctantly after a whole hour we set off once more, undecided whether to stop at Claverdon – only one mile away – or go off into the blue with uncertain B & B prospects. In the event, the matter was decided for us. As we walked towards Claverdon we passed a house with a big front garden. In the front path was a wheelbarrow full of garden rubbish, on top of which sat an extraordinary old gentleman wearing a large white cowboy hat, dirty trousers, and displaying white whiskers and beard and long white hair. This – we were to discover quite soon – was Bill O'Brian, a flamboyant and very articulate Irishman. When he saw us he got off his wheelbarrow, leaned on the gate and started asking us lots of questions. The answers he got so obviously intrigued him that he opened the gate and invited us in for tea. When we reached the front door he started shouting to his wife – who was upstairs – that there were two people for tea and they must have some of her rhubarb pie. The poor lady came downstairs startled and slightly bemused. Meanwhile old Bill had brought us into an untidy sitting room, where he started laying a table with a tablecloth and knives and forks. By this time, Grace (Mrs O'Brian) had begun to enter into the spirit of the thing, put the kettle on, and produced two pieces of the most gorgeous rhubarb pie we've ever tasted. 'Aren't I having any?' asks Bill. 'No', she replies. 'Why?' asks he. 'You'll have to wait until I make another.' Oh dear! she'd given us the last two pieces. However, as he was still loudly demanding food, she went into the kitchen and brought back an enormous fruit cake, and a huge slab of butter, both of which we were pressed to accept. Their conversation about each other was very funny. Bill referred to her when speaking to us as 'she'. 'All *she* can do well is to make fruit cake.' Grace did the same. '*He* pulls up my plants thinking they are weeds.' We heard all about their family, Bill's views on the Irish question, how the government ought to tackle the problems of mine closures and many other deep subjects, until finally we said we really should go or we'd never get to John o' Groats. (Bill was looking much tidier, as he had disappeared upstairs soon after he had brought us into the house and returned washed and changed into clean trousers.) We shook each other warmly by the hand and set off northwards once more. A fascinating episode in our pilgrimage.

By this time it was far too late to go further than the next village, so we called in at the only shop to enquire about accommodation. We were directed to Mrs Bromilow at Woodside (just down the road). It turned out to be over a mile in the wrong direction. Here we are, sitting bathed and changed, in a beautiful garden, with a bluebell wood the like of which we have never seen, outside our bedroom window. We are being fed, which is an added bonus. It seems expensive, but we are glad not to have to go out, and there's nowhere near anyway. We are right out in the country. It couldn't be more unlike our stay in Stratford where cars were hurtling past all night. The only sound is the cuckoo. With all the interruptions we have only walked seven miles today. It will be a long day tomorrow.

Day 34 – 22nd May – Wednesday

A marvellous night's sleep in this peaceful place. We were late going to bed (10.45 pm). Doreen Bromilow came into the sitting room, where we'd had a very simple supper (cold meat, salad, egg custard and fruit, £9 each), and talked to us the whole evening. She is a widow with two sons, one of whom we met who is divorced and lives in London – computer man. The other went out to South Africa, met a SA girl and settled there. Daughter, also in London, married with one baby. She goes out to work so cannot have another. Mrs B. opens her gardens to the public once a year (Bluebell Sunday) to share it and to raise money for good causes. She has 17 acres of woodland, part of which with its carpet of bluebells, comes almost up to our bedroom window. There are many rare trees in the wood, and an organisation – a smaller version of the National Trust – provides guides to show people round. Mrs Bromilow, with helpers from the village, provides continuous food, including hot lunches, on the open day. She and her architect husband came here 42 years ago when they married. The house was built in 1918 but he did a lot of alterations to it. It is quite attractive, but the real glory is the magnificent garden.

12.30 pm – Lowsonford – sitting beside a canal where all the holiday barges are tied up. After we left the bluebell wood we got lost down a bridle path. Retracing our steps uphill, we tried again. Finding no directions in one hamlet we called at a farm but there was no-one in. Knocked on the door of a big house (very opulent, garages for 3 cars) – only dogs in. So we trudged on in roughly the right direction on a muddy bridlepath. Coming onto a minor road at last we found a living human being (in fact two) who told us where we were and directed us to this pub. One of the men overtook us in his car and gave us a thumbnail sketch of his companion whose father had come down from South Shields on the Jarrow Marches – stayed and founded a firm making car radiators, became a wealthy man, died three years ago and left his son a million (the son hadn't worked since). If we'd known all this we would have asked for a donation for CA.

As we walked over the bridge here we watched a narrow canal boat go through the lock gates which was fascinating.

No sandwiches here – so we are having a salad between us.

6.10 pm. – We have arrived at our destination – a farm which Herbert booked by telephone en route this afternoon. The farmer has left a note in the letter box saying he will be back soon, so we are sitting in the sunshine in his garden. It has been quite an interesting afternoon. We soon found 'The Way' after leaving the pub, but encountered a number of hazards thereafter. At one point the stile we should have used was standing in deep water. Further up the field there was an electric fence. Eventually we crawled on our tummies under the fence, only to find we were in deep bog. Then we were again embroiled in an electric fence and a herd of cows chased us, so altogether it was quite exciting. But not so exciting as tonight's B & B. Externally it is very attractive three-storeyed farmhouse. But inside . . . The owner, who turned up soon after we had arrived, is not a farmer as we had assumed but a self-styled 'financier'. He opened the door and we were aghast. The hall was not only dirty, dark and musty, but full of boxes of papers, typewriters, empty bottles and other rubbish. He offered us two rooms – each with a single bed. Only one was made up. There was some weird literature in the bookcase of the better of the two rooms, which concerned us. The 'dining room' where presumably we will have breakfast (and which we investigated after our host had departed for Coventry 'on business') is a mess. It all looks as though he has just moved in, but he said he had been there 15 years. He mentioned his wife, but there has been no sign of her. The bathwater was cold, there were no towels and no wastepaper basket. Of course we have been terribly spoilt, but this is certainly a great comedown.

So we have come out to 'the local' to eat and we will stay until bedtime, then go back and squeeze into the single bed. We should be prepared for these shocks. We say that we must have our ups and downs and we have had our experiences of these in past walks, but this is very strange. Why has he accepted us? Why is he on the official list and yet had no sort of indication outside his house of B & B? In fact he can only offer two single bedrooms, with no hot water, no tea, no telly? Why is the house in complete turmoil and bits of ancient vehicles lying around the garden? Perhaps all will be revealed: perhaps it won't.

When we returned from the pub we found the toilet had leaked – there was water all over the floor which had stained the carpet bright blue. The hot water tap did not function, and the eerie silence of the lonely house began to take its toll on us. Herbert said, 'I'm not happy, I don't think we should stay here.' After a debate about this we decided to pack up and go before our host returned. We left him a note to say we were very sorry but we really couldn't stay there, and set off down the dark country lane, rather like two naughty children afraid of being found out, and without the slightest idea what we were going to do. The only thing we could think of was to return to the pub to see if they had accommodation. In we went, and Herbert was just being told by the barmaid that they did not take people for the night when a voice behind me said, 'Do you always bring your packs with you when you go out to eat?' It was the gentleman himself – who had told us he was going to Coventry thirty miles away. We both looked at him speechless. Then Herbert muttered lamely that we'd decided to go because his wife wasn't happy (it was he who wasn't happy). Philip – the odd gentleman's name – seemed genuinely upset that we had nowhere to sleep. We told him nothing worked and he said he would take us back in his car and 'sort things out'. Before we knew what was happening he had stuffed our packs into the boot of his car so we had no option but to return with him to the place we had been so glad to escape from. Philip was indeed very anxious to put things right. He agreed the toilet was leaking and the hot tap didn't produce hot water, although he said the shower was working perfectly, and anyway he hadn't known anything about these deficiencies. He suggested moving the bed out of the offending room and putting it beside the other bed which he'd already offered us. There was a bathroom near which was perfectly all right he assured us, and immediately began lugging the bed and bedding along the corridor. By this time we were so pussy struck we just gave in. So we had a bed to sleep in after all, although we were somewhat disturbed by the proximity of Birmingham flight path and the squawking of the goose which was kept penned up in the garden. Also there were many mysterious noises of people coming and going, talking and laughing somewhere in the big old house, although we never saw anybody except our odd friend.

The Goose That Squawked

Breakfast was downstairs in another untidy room, served by our host. This room had a disconnected freezer standing in the middle, and a microwave, also unattached, on a bench. The large and ancient fireplace was stuffed with old rubbish like the entrance hall. The kitchen seemed to be upstairs, and Philip produced some scrambled eggs which seemed to be his entire repertoire. He told us he had a mentally handicapped son, that he had an office in Gerrards Cross, that all the piles of papers in the drab and dirty hall had been in another office. The story of his life, he said, would take all day to recount, but we sensed a tragedy somewhere. By this time we were sorry for Philip, and when we left we shook him warmly by the hand and thanked him for his hospitality.

The thing we have noticed about The Heart of England Way is that we never meet anyone either in the villages, which are deserted, or on the footpaths. The exception was at a National Trust Elizabethan house yesterday where there was a full car park and lots of old ladies and a few old men wandering around. We showed our National Trust cards in order to get in, not to see the mansion but to get some much needed tea. It's extraordinary how we are able to accelerate after drinking the divine liquid.

Day 35 – 23rd May – Thursday

4.00 pm. Shustoke.

Our guardian angel is still looking after us. Herbert has been very concerned about the lack of accommodation, and we had been walking all day without seeing anything. We decided to go on to the next village which involved a long straight road, and intended to enquire at the post office. When we reached it, we turned the corner and there was the post office sign, but displaying a large B & B. The postmaster told us he wasn't starting officially as he was waiting for a licence, but he didn't turn us away. This is a listed building (1540), newly painted; beautiful and new rose pink carpets help us to forget the disaster of yesterday. (As we were looking anxiously for a B & B sign today we saw on the long, boring road, a notice in the distance. What were we to be offered? – Charcoal – 3 kilos £1.99, 5 kilos £3.99. The same old story.)

We are both tired and aching tonight and looking forward to three days' rest at Carr House. Teresa, our landlady tonight, is a pretty girl. She is a teacher in Birmingham. Besides running the B & B she and her husband also own the old manor house next door; they have a tea shop as well and are helped by their son. The husband keeps the post office and general store. What energy! The family live behind the post office in the old manor house. It was all 15th century with original fireplaces and blackened beams. Sadly modern buildings have encroached on all sides of it.

Day 36 – 24th May – Friday

Slept in. Very good breakfast served by Teresa's son. She left early to go to her job. The children she teaches are very badly behaved apparently. I wonder why she doesn't concentrate on her B & B and restaurant. It was quite expensive we found, especially as there were no extras such as PFs (Private Facilities), TV, tea/coffee.

Today our walk has taken us through fields at first, then a rather urban landscape. England is changing from the agriculture and old farmhouses to more ordinary architecture, flat countryside and signs of industry.

3.30 pm. – On the train between Tamworth and Sheffield.

Today we diverted along the canal towpaths which made a nice change from the road. A man on a mobile cutter was cutting the grass so there was a fragrant scent as we walked. Nearly 400 miles now. And a weekend's rest to look forward to at Carr House. We are both ready for a break. Let's hope we won't be too much bother to them.

Day 37 – 28th May – Tuesday

After laying up for three days we are on the road again. I'm damaged after a fall from a racer bike, but was expertly dealt with at the Sheffield Hospital casualty department and fortunately I can still walk. Today dawned dull and dry – typical Pennine cloud. We left Sheffield at 10.18 am, arrived Tamworth 11.30 am. Road walking for 2–3 miles; stopped at a pub at 12.45 pm. No food, so had cider and Jane's cheese and biscuits. The scenery and architecture here are uninteresting, although once we regained the Heart of England Way there were some quite attractive brick farmhouses. A few pigs were grazing in the fields beside the cows. Avoided 'extreme danger' – a notice advising us not to venture into a quarry, especially in fog. 'The Way' merged with the main road to Lichfield which we saw on the road sign indicating the city was the birthplace of Dr Johnson. After walking through a labyrinth of modern housing estates we reached the centre of the city, which was an improvement. We found the Tourist Office and are now installed in a Georgian house in the city centre. No PFs, not even a washbasin, although there is an elegant Victorian jug and basin on a marble washstand. The room is big, airy and clean and we are resting our feet, glad to be out of the new boots which we bought on Saturday. The wornout ones have gone to be resoled.

Day 38 – 29th May – Wednesday

A slow start. Our young hostess, Abby, is a student looking after the house while her mother is on holiday. She was nervous about accepting visitors, but her mother had told her she could have any money she earned, so she took a chance. She gave us breakfast of fruit, brown toast, elegantly served in a high ceilinged dining room with a magnificent cut glass chandelier. A bookcase on the wall was stacked with books of all descriptions. Last night's meal was another highlight. We walked to a hotel a few yards up the road, and were given melon, salmon and strawberries.

This morning began badly. We returned to the Tourist Office who couldn't help us with accommodation in Rugeley – our destination today. We then shopped for something for lunch and had a quick look at the cathedral. This is a very grand and ornate edifice in the local red stone. Carved figures and flying buttresses on the exterior. Three steeples, many stained-glass windows.

We rejoined the Heart of England Way but very soon lost it – why? Because the sign had been vandalised. After walking a couple of miles in the wrong direction, we waylaid some passers-by who put us right. It had taken us 1½ hours to do half a mile. After that we made better progress, although once again the sign was completely hidden by a pile of farm rubbish. (Was this deliberate?) Some gorgeous tiny foals in one field were photographed. We had a glass of cider at a pub – taken outside so that we could eat our picnic. Then we were on minor roads, forest roads and a long descent into Rugeley. We came to a dreary town centre, wondering where to look for a bed, when suddenly across the road was the Little Chef Travelodge – just what we wanted. Alas, they were fully booked, but the receptionist phoned a nearby hotel who could take us; she also rang for a taxi to take us there. The Cedar Tree Hotel – more expensive than the Travelodge and not so nice. Well, that's life!

The weather has continued dry and overcast. The sun did peep out for a few minutes but soon gave up. The high level walk into this town was quite spectacular, but most of the day has been spent walking through fields full of buttercups, on minor roads lined with may blossom or on forest paths. We have left Warwickshire and are now in the county of Staffordshire – the Potteries. Herbert spends nearly all his time anxiously studying maps, measuring distances, and trying to work out where we can stay. It's a great labour.

Day 39 – 30th May – Thursday

Driest, dullest May on record. Today it continues to be dull and dry. We are lucky to have had so little rain, but we would love some sunshine. We have finished the Heart of England Way and today are beginning the Staffordshire Way. Herbert has booked up the next two nights but after that there is a problem. We were intending to go out into the wilds of Derbyshire but as there is no accommodation we have had to change to 'plan B' and go on roads to Buxton.

4.30 pm. Arrived at the Hill Crest Guest House, Uttoxeter. We returned by taxi this morning to our point of departure then set off to find the Staffordshire Way. The cooling towers and chimneys of Rugeley power station were belching forth their poison into the already very gloomy and overcast sky so we were glad to leave the town. Again we lost our way and enquired at a lonely and derelict farmhouse. An old Welshman told us we were on his private drive but allowed us to go on – showing us the way to the right track. 'Just follow the cows.' Once we found the sign we were all right.

The way led us mostly through fields with dozens of stiles, and we found a nice little pub for lunch in Abbots Bromley. Then it was fields and pretty minor roads until the outskirts of Uttoxeter where the Guest House is. The most unexpectedly sweet scent accompanied us for most of the afternoon. To our surprise we realised the fragrance came from the flowers of the broad beans which filled field after field.

Our good fortune continues and we haven't had to go out for a meal. Afterwards our hostess took us for a drive to see a bronze sculpture – 'The Startled Horse' which is life size. This is in the grounds of the JCB headquarters and is very impressive.

We managed to contact Nigel (my nephew) who said he will try to meet us in Buxton. He had asked 'his people' (BBC North West) about publicity, but as we were from the North East they weren't interested.

In the visitors book of this guest house was an entry – July 17th 1990 – J MacArthur. ('Mac' – who had given us so much help in planning.)

Day 40 – 31st May – Friday *Another* dull, dry day.

I reckon this is not only the driest May, but also the most sunless on record. We are off to Alton today along the Staffordshire Way. We saw 'The Way' last night on our car ride and it looked very pretty. We have been promised some sun this afternoon by the weatherman. This guest house is quite full. There are another eight people here – four Japanese, four English.

Our hosts have donated the cost of the meal to CA. The first donation for a few weeks. Our hostess wanted me to take some of her homemade damson jam, but it was too heavy. Lunch in Rocester – pronounced Roaster. Dreary place, dreary weather. Walked through fields again after losing our way as we do every morning just now. These were full of wild geese and goslings, flying heron and pheasants. We passed through a posh clay pigeon shooting club – warned by red flag and sounds of shots to keep to paths (Club accepted no responsibility for personal injury).

PM. Difficult. Followed public footpath sign, traversed a large boggy area with the aid of a big stick, only to find our way completely barred by nettles, briars and barbed wire. Had to retrace our steps, taking another path. This one was blocked by electric fence. Herbert was very disgusted with the Staffordshire Way. We returned to the road. After a while another public footpath sign appeared. This was clear and we arrived safely in Alton – to the sounds of merriment coming from some hills ahead of us which, being covered with trees, obscured the source. This was the famous Alton Towers – the biggest fun park in Europe, we were told. A mini Disneyland in fact. Entrance fee £10.50 – no thank you.

We found the B & B we had booked. It was above a shop and run by Pakistanis. I am ashamed to say we rejected it – *not* because of racism, but lack of facilities. Two rooms – both occupied, shared bath, washbasin and loo (all in one room). So we are at the Bulls Head, down the street. We have a very nice room with PFs, quiet, clean and we can eat here so that's a blessing. It won't be a meal like last night, I expect. In accordance with doctor's instructions, I have taken (or rather soaked) off my bandage except for the last little piece of gauze. So that crisis is over.

Day 41 – 1st June – Saturday The usual cold, grey day.

We had a rather noisy night as we were directly above the bar. The poor landlord has to put up with it every night. Today we go to Leek where we may meet Nigel. The Bulls Head is a pleasant place. They kindly dried our socks for us last night and turned down pop music when we asked, and what is more they gave us fresh fruit salad for breakfast.

Flashback to yesterday – we passed a cotton mill at Rocester with a plaque saying Richard Arkwright inventor of the spinning jenny worked there.

12.30pm. The clouds are lifting and the sun has been trying to shine – the first time for a week. After a brief return to the Bulls Head (to return the room key) we have had an easy and pleasant walk, first along a path made out of a disused railway, then, great excitement, along the actual track. It had been in use until a couple of years ago and all the rails and sleepers are still intact, although weeds and wild flowers are rapidly taking over. We met one couple walking in the opposite direction, otherwise we've been alone as usual. Where are all the people in this country? In the supermarkets perhaps. We are now at the Railway Hotel having our usual snack lunch.

4.45 pm. Arrived in Leek. It has been a lovely afternoon. The sun got out after lunch and the countryside was transformed. We resumed our walk along the sleepers for a mile or so, then went through a gate to the canal which was on a higher level than the railway. It was a pleasant towpath – not too straight to become monotonous, with wonderful reflections of trees in the still water and some colourful long boats moored alongside from time to time. After we left the canal we stopped to see if the pub which advertised teas would give us any. No joy. We continued on our way – greatly diverted by the sight of a low loader carrying a railway carriage for the nearby railway museum. The lorry had broken down, blocking the entire road and railway crossing. Cars were piling up behind, but there was room for two walkers to squeeze past. Herbert took a photograph of the scene. Then it was uphill across fields until we met a road which would give us a short cut to Leek. A pretty road with colourful hedgerows and lined with immense beech trees – the first we had seen since Devon – made the time pass quickly. There was a long steep climb, then a long descent to the main road into Leek. We were tired by then, and longing for tea. Lacking this vital liquid we sat on a seat and shared an apple.

Our 'hotel' is decidedly rundown, but we have a clean, sunny room and a bath, and the owner, having previously said he couldn't give us a meal, has relented, so we won't have to go out. And, surprise, surprise, just after we'd bathed, and were not yet dressed, Nigel ran up the stairs and knocked on our door. The whole family had come to see us. The three children are well behaved and just sat quietly drinking lemonade while we grown-ups chatted. Now we are looking forward to a meal.

8.45 pm. In bed. We had a nice meal, but were quite alone in a vast, cold and dreary dining room.

Day 42 – 2nd June – Sunday

We had a long talk with the proprietor's wife before we left. She is a Portuguese lady, her husband is Welsh. She was very concerned, as so many older people seem to be, at the drop in standards. Children are spoilt, badly behaved, no respect for anyone, she said. Told us how much better Portugal had been under a dictatorship. People were quite safe in the streets – there was a policeman at both ends to enforce order (but she didn't say *how* it was enforced). Under the socialists law and order has gone. Thefts are commonplace.

We left at 10 am and started the 12-mile hike into Buxton along the A53. It was a pleasant road to begin with, and much enlivened by the sight of hundreds of cyclists who, we learned on enquiry, were taking part in a triathlon event. This involved cycling 12 miles over hilly roads, then swimming half a mile across a lake and finally running round it. It began to rain soon after we started walking so it was miserable for the cyclists (and walkers). We met one poor girl pushing her bike. She had become dizzy and thought she had better give up. She was frozen, but there were ambulances and lots of people in cars looking for casualties so she would be picked up.

The weather deteriorated as we walked (yesterday must have been a one off) and soon we were in fog as well as rain, although this was probably cloud as we climbed to 1,540 ft. Having passed one attractive-looking pub, as it was only 12 o'clock we plodded on for over an hour without seeing another. At one point we saw a notice advising us not to touch anything by the roadside as it might explode and kill us. How very remarkable. Eventually we came across a grotty pub which could only provide limited sustenance, but at least we had a rest and got warm. We continued along the same road, narrowly missing death through careless driving in such low visibility. We reached Buxton earlier than we expected and soon found a B & B. As often happened, we were told firmly *no* evening meal, so we asked if we might have our breakfast this evening instead of tomorrow. The lady – Cindy – was hesitant at first, but then agreed. Here we are installed in a room which is the best for some time. PF, TV, two armchairs, spacious, pretty and spotless. The house was built in the gracious days before the first World War and has an air of great elegance. Our wet clothes plus rucksacks, are in a warm cellar and we are going to have bacon and eggs at 6 pm. What adventures we do have. My feet are sore today, which is a nuisance, but they'll be better after a rest.

7.45 pm. We've had our breakfast – bacon, 2 eggs, 2 sausages, tomatoes, waffle potato, tea, rice pudding (for Herbert) and bread and jam. We spoke to Jane who will meet us on Tuesday. Radio Manchester wants to get hold of us, also Radio Carlisle. We were spotted by the Whitburn postman today.

We crossed into Derbyshire today and have now finished with the Staffordshire Way. We pick up the Cestrian Link Way on the far side of Buxton. My cheap watch has given up and will have to be replaced.

Day 43 – 3rd June – Monday. 9 am Sunny (so far).

We are going to have a look at the town then on to the Peak Forest.

5.50 pm. Castleton. We decided to go on a bit, and in spite of a gloomy weather report there was very little rain. But it is cold. It was a pleasant walk into Buxton – our digs were on the outskirts – and we had coffee at the famous Pavilion which is approached through a vast conservatory of exotic trees and flowers. It was uphill on the far side of the town but there were good views from the top – wide vistas and rolling hills. We passed huge limestone quarries with bright green artificial lakes, which – we were told – were used for washing the limestone. We lunched in a little pub beside the quarry and the landlord lit a coal fire especially for us. Arriving in Peak Forest we decided to move on as it was only 2 o'clock. Then began the long climb over the hills and steep descent into Castleton. We met no hikers, one cyclist and about 100 young women all wearing very long skirts and trainers. They looked Arabic. Castleton is a touristy place, full of tea shops, craft shops, souvenir shops, etc. There aren't many B & Bs and most were full. But we have been lucky. We have the last room in one of them. It is quite a nice room (though not to compare with last night) but so far the bathroom has been occupied and our bedroom is on the ground floor with windows overlooking the street which is a little awkward. We decided to eat before changing so went to a cafe round the corner and had a satisfactory meal. The press has found us and want to write an article about us.

Tomorrow we meet Jane, and it is Carr House for the next few nights which will be a great help with the finances. The name of our refuge tonight is 'The Ramblers Rest'.

We are in much more varied countryside after the flat dullness of the Heart of England and Staffs Ways. We did not see much of it on the A53 to Buxton because we were lost in the fog which, so local inhabitants told us, envelops the moors for at least a quarter of the year. Buxton itself is in a most beautiful position, set in a bowl surrounded with hills. Despite the 1,000 ft altitude there are plenty of trees and vegetation. The walk over from Peak Forest to Castleton was typical limestone country, with white outcrops, white dry-stone walls criss-crossing the landscape, and bright green grass. The last mile or so comes down a steep path through a limestone gulley, with caves, sheer cliffs and a very dramatic castle, Percival Castle, built in 1086 by William the Conqueror's son, perched on the top overhanging the gulley. We know this variety won't last long because soon it is the Pennine Way which will be like the surface of the moon.

Day 44 – 4th June – Tuesday Fine and sunny, but poor weather forecast.

There is snow on the hills. It was a lovely morning. The landscape was marred by a large cement works but the walk uphill out of Castleton with tree-covered hills, was wonderful. There were hang gliders to entertain us as we walked. As we began the descent we saw Jane coming up to meet us. She led us across fields and over stiles to the car where a picnic was waiting. Also, unfortunately a flat tyre. Jane and Herbert changed this, then we had our picnic, at which point we were joined by a very talkative stranger. Next came a visit to the boot shop to ask advice about our problem (with my new boots) – none was forthcoming. Back to Carr House, and after supper we had a rare treat – a visit to the Crucible Theatre in Sheffield to see 'Measure for Measure'.

Day 45 – 5th June – Wednesday A bright sunny morning and a very early start.

With Gillian for company we started walking at 9 am. Jane dropped us at our arrival point of yesterday. This was our first day on the much feared Pennine Way, and in Herbert's words it has been an 'unmitigated disaster'. We missed the vital turning early on and got completely lost. Up and down, round and round, with Herbert and Gillian arguing about which was the right way. Eventually, after four hours walking, we plotted our route by a reservoir which led us to the elusive Pennine Way. It was then too late to make our rendezvous with Jane, so we continued on the path we were on, hoping to reach a telephone before Jane left her office at 3.15 pm. We did not. We rang Keith – no reply.

Sitting in the pub on Snake Pass we asked for tea. No tea, only coffee. But we would like tea. 'You'd better go for a walk and find somewhere else,' was the unsympathetic reply. A bit hard after walking from Land's End. But there are some nice people around. Two young men sitting drinking beer asked us if we'd had a good walk. 'No, we got lost.' Then we told them the story of Jane waiting for us some miles away. 'We'll drive you there,' one of them said. So Herbert and Gillian have gone with them, while I am waiting here in case Jane turns up at this pub. We have certainly walked more than 10 miles today, but have only reduced the distance to John o' Groats by about four or five. Herbert is very disappointed.

We have been lucky with the weather. In spite of their bad

reputation, the Pennines have remained dry today, and we have even had some sun with a brisk wind blowing. The ground is dry which is a great mercy, but the bare hills, stony paths and featureless landscape with its monotonous peat bogs and moorland, quite devoid of life except for some very dirty sheep, provide more of an endurance test than enjoyment. There are plenty of people on the actual Pennine Way but today we have only crossed it, without having walked on it. As it is the only way to go north apart from the M6 or A1 we must persevere for a few days until we reach Settle.

5.30 pm. Jane, Herbert and Gillian arrived at the inn to pick me up. Jane had climbed a hill to meet us and had returned to the car just as Herbert and Gillian turned up with the two 'good samaritans'. Arriving at Carr House just after six our kind daughter made us tea and then sent us up to have a bath. Alas! her labours were not over even then. Herbert wasn't happy about the scar on my knee, so Jane took us back to the Sheffield hospital for some expert attention. All was well. I was seen quickly, rebandaged and we were back in less than an hour. But we were all – especially Jane – worn out, and went straight to bed.

Day 46 – 6th June – Thursday We awoke to thick fog.

That settled it. We were definitely not going to risk getting lost among the peat bogs of the Pennine Way. Gillian has exams today so there's no pressure on us to keep up with her fast young legs. We left Carr House at 8.15 am – these terrible early starts are necessary in order to allow Jane to get to work after delivering us – and Jane drove us to the bottom of Snake Pass. It is now nearly 11.30 am and we made good progress until . . . Herbert was putting a plaster on my foot (what a nuisance I am) and to do so had to take off his map case and camera. He forgot to pick them up. Once he discovered the loss he hurried back up the hill. A cyclist has just stopped and told me he had found them and was going to take them to the police when he saw Herbert and gave them to him. What good people there are in the world. So now I am sitting on a stone waiting for him to return.

3.15 pm. We are early today for our meeting with Jane. We are at Crowden where we are to meet her at 3.30. After the crisis of the lost camera, map, and cheque book, Herbert was very tired as he had climbed back up the steep Snake Pass at top speed. He must have looked all in when he reached me because a driver stopped to ask if he was all right.

We walked into Glossop and had a welcome drink and sandwich. Once again it was a climb out of the town on the other side. We managed a short cut through some fields to the reservoir and we are sitting beside the very noisy Huddersfield road, part of which we must walk along tomorrow. Let's hope the clouds lift and we will be able to tackle the Pennine Way again. It is just about impossible in mist as it is so badly marked.

Day 47 – 7th June – Friday

Disaster! The clouds were right down this morning. Jane and Gillian drove us up to Saddleworth Moor where we were to pick up the Pennine Way. It was difficult enough for Jane to drive; walking across the Pennines was impossible. So plan B was put into operation and we walked down the road into Crowden – a route we should have taken in reverse the next day. It was cold and miserable, but at least we were making some progress and our 'shepherds' met us at intervals in the car with food and drink. We managed eight miles in total and at that point had done 23 of the 60 miles of the Pennine Way we had to walk. We were driven back to Carr House and hot baths. What were we to do if the weather didn't improve? Visions of vast detours through Huddersfield and Bradford loomed before us. The Parkins all went to the theatre: we were glad to stay by the fire on a bitterly cold night. Is it really June?

Day 48 – 8th June – Saturday

A miracle – we awoke to see a bright blue sky. Everyone was up with the lark. Rain was forecast for the afternoon. Keith and David went to Headingley, Gillian to play in a concert, Jane, our faithful shepherd drove us back to Saddleworth and for the first time we were actually on the Pennine Way. It is now 2.45 pm. We have another 10 miles behind us and have had an easy and pleasant walk, much of it high up with extensive views. The ground was dry – after the first boggy section (Herbert went in up to his knees). Jane has met us every three miles or wherever the Pennine Way crossed a road. A mobile cafe provided us with tea for our picnic, after which we climbed a hill and crossed the elegant footbridge over the M62 which was a thrill. We met two walkers who shook us warmly by the hand when they heard the full extent of our walk. We have seen only three Pennine Way walkers in all. Tomorrow we will be on our own again. We'll miss 'the good shepherd'.

Saddleworth

Day 49 – 9th June – Sunday Dry, with high cloud, no fog thank goodness.

We had another early start (we have been up at 7 am while at Carr House). Three Parkins went off to Headingley and Jane drove us to the White House where we had finished yesterday. The distance in the car (a journey of $1\frac{1}{2}$ hours) reminded us how far we had come since Tuesday when we had met Jane near Castleton. There was a hurricane blowing when we disembarked, and we put on all our Goretex. We got a little warmer as we walked, but it began to rain heavily. We have had another easy, fairly level walk on the Pennine Way today. We missed the worst part the day the clouds came down (Day 46) and when we went on the road. It was a high level walk today, at first beside a reservoir (there are reservoirs all over this part of Yorkshire, and they are all full – I wonder why?) then on an escarpment with wonderful views down the Calder valley. The ugly monument, put up in 1841 to commemorate the first victory over Napoleon, created a diversion. We climbed a narrow dark spiral staircase inside it to a viewing balcony where we were blasted by wind and rain. Some schoolgirls obligingly shone a torch to save us from falling down the stairs in the inky blackness. After this we made our way downhill to Hebden Bridge, our destination for tonight. The last part of the descent was through trees, which made a change from the bleak moorland. It had been too wet to eat Jane's sandwiches so we plodded along an uninteresting road until, simultaneously, the rain stopped, the sun came out, and a seat in a tiny public garden appeared. We should be used to these surprises by now, they are always happening. The gilt on the gingerbread was the unexpected view across the road of a window through which a telly could be clearly seen, and the Test Match was on.

The rain began again as we continued into the town. Although it is Sunday there is great activity. Nearly all the shops and cafes are open. People and cars crowded together made a complete contrast with the empty moorland we have left. The Tourist Office has directed us to the Hebden Lodge Hotel, and we are now having a rest in a comfortable room before going out for high tea (we don't want the hotel's elaborate and expensive dinner) and church. We passed the Hebden Methodist church as we walked through. It seems to be a very modern building.

10.15 pm. There was communion at the service. The Minister, who was playing a guitar, asked if anyone would like to choose a hymn. Herbert chose 'Father I place into your hands the things I cannot do' – very appropriate. Afterwards we had supper at an Italian restaurant which was nothing special. We rang Helen who is lonely without Rob. She has no idea when he will get home. We watched Tinker Tailor. Night, night. (It's still pouring.)

Day 50 – 10th June – Monday Very gloomy weather forecast, but at 9.15 am it is not raining yet.

Today we go off into the wilderness.

6.30 pm. We have had a rough passage today. It began well with a steep, but very rewarding footpath out of Hebden Bridge until we had achieved 1,000 ft. There were extensive views down to the valley below and over to the hills we had climbed down yesterday. On one of these we could just make out the outline of the monument we climbed yesterday. At the top of the hill we reached Heptenstall which is a perfectly preserved and unspoilt Yorkshire village. The main street, in fact the only street, is cobbled, and there were no cars to be seen as no through traffic is allowed. We went into the quaint post office to buy cards and the postmistress asked us about our journey. When we told her, she opened her till and gave us a ten pound note. We had a look round the village then continued uphill until we found our old friend (or enemy), the Pennine Way, once more. After that we had many hours of struggle in wind and rain across bleak moorland, most of it uphill. We passed a derelict farmhouse which it is believed was the inspiration for Wuthering Heights. A plaque on the wall told us that the farmhouse, even when complete, was quite unlike the one Emily Bronte described, but that she may have been influenced by its situation high up on the barren, windswept hillside. A savage wind howled ceaselessly through the few trees surrounding it. At last we began to go downhill which made life easier, until we reached another reservoir and saw a sign

'Ponden Hall $\frac{1}{4}$ mile'. That meant another climb.

We are now installed in Ponden Hall, and it is one of the most extraordinary places we have ever stayed in. It is a 17th century building and, according to Wainwright, *really* is the Thrushcross Grange of Wuthering Heights. Wainwright also says it has been preserved in its original character. I'll say! It has probably retained its original decorations as well. We were greeted by a little girl of about ten who led us through a stone flagged hall which was full of odds and ends, into a huge room with a big black stove, an enormous dining table, and various settees and armchairs the covers of which were full of holes. There was a spinning wheel in one corner which the child, after giving us a cup of tea, proceeded to work, spinning some wool she had collected from the fields. Another girl – an older sister – who had bare feet, started chopping wood with an axe, and then lit the stove. An angelic little boy (who, we discovered, is the big sister's child) took Herbert into the kitchen to see the telly (Test Match). The kitchen is a jumble like the rest of the house. The ten-year-old took us up to see our room which is a real joke. There are big holes in the carpet; the wallpaper has an antique design of pink and blue flowers; the end of the wooden bed wobbles violently when touched; there is a marble washstand with a big china bowl and jug full of plastic lilac. An ancient spotted oval mirror hangs on the wall, but there is a modern and very warm heater – which is a godsend as the weather is perishing. A wooden cradle on rockers stands beneath the window. Through this window we can see the trees bending in the wind, and can almost imagine Cathy's ghost trying to get in. Beyond are the bleak hills which stretch for miles in all directions. Behind our bed is a large picture of Mr Gladstone who surveys us sternly. Vast rooms go in all directions. The one next to ours has a polished wooden floor and is big enough for a ballroom. Another contains an enormous quantity of clothes hanging along a long pole. Everywhere in the house there are notices in a child's hand, for example, 'My Mum says will you let her know at bedtime if you don't want a cooked breakfast, or if you want a vegetarian breakfast'. We have yet to see Mum.

So far it seems the place is run by this child and her older sister.

9.20 pm. In bed! Surprisingly in view of the unpromising surroundings, we have had a very good meal of cauliflower soup, roast chicken, baked potatoes, lots of vegetables and a salad, plum and apple crumble, coffee with cream and all for £7. Marvellous! We sat at the long refectory table with the other guests who were all walkers except for one elderly couple searching for their family tree. One of the walkers, a solitary male, had made footprints which we had followed all day. A young couple from Quebec, English not Canadian, have come over the Atlantic especially to walk the Pennine Way. It was a very friendly gathering.

We went into the kitchen afterwards and met Mum – a very cheerful lady – and thanked her for the meal.

We have no washbasin in our funny room so there may be problems in the morning. The toilet arrangements here are quite comic. The bathroom – with plenty of hot water – has a

Ponden Hall

floor which is coming adrift in the middle. When you try to unbolt the door on leaving the bolt falls on the floor. The only other available 'facility' has a hook to close the door which leaves a big gap through which the current occupant can be clearly seen.

Day 51 – 11th June – Tuesday

At 7.00 am, on visiting the bathroom, I met our hostess leaving it clad only in a towel. She smiled cheerfully at me as we met. One bedroom (the door was open) contains six beds which is advertised at the entrance as dormitory accommodation. Today is dull but mercifully dry. We have had a homemade breakfast, in good company – brown wholemeal bread, homemade lemon curd.

1.00 pm. The Black Bull, Vowling. We left Ponden Hall at 10.00 am and walked in wind and rain over more bleak and boggy moorland which, after an initial climb, was mostly level: then a long descent into this village. We have seen no other walkers. Our friends of last night will be way ahead of us and there is no-one following us. Hot soup stoked us up for what was to be a gruelling afternoon. On leaving the pub we asked a man working on the road to direct us to the Pennine Way, which he did, adding in a thick Irish brogue, 'There's some toilets up there if you want them.' After lunch it was up and down four times, across wet fields and moors and roads in a strong, very cold wind. Eventually we saw a cluster of houses in the distance, high up on yet another hill. This was our destination for tonight. It seemed miles away, but Mr Wainwright assured us it was but one mile distant. We went on through a filthy farmyard, up a steep road and arrived in a pretty Dales village (award winning we are told). We soon found Elm Tree House and were given a warm welcome. Our hostess had just turned someone away saying the room was booked, so she was pleased we'd turned up. She gave us scones for tea which were most welcome. This is an early Georgian house – 1730. It is a stone building with elegant sash windows, not so old as Ponden Hall, but much cleaner.

Day 52 – 12th June – Wednesday Thornton in Craven. Clear at 6.00 am, cloudy by 9.00 am, with a poor forecast.

Mrs Davey took us to the nearest pub as she couldn't offer us a meal and collected us later. Back in her house we sat beside a real fire until bedtime. Breakfast was in a beautiful dining room with another coal fire. We met a couple from Norfolk.

12.45 pm. The Old Forge, Gargrave (Gargrave, according to Wainwright is 'a sophisticated place' as it boasts public conveniences). We are lunching here in a craft shop full of things which we cannot carry and do not want to buy anyway. We have had a pleasant morning; there has been some sunshine, with a brisk but cold wind. Part of the way was along a tow path. The canal came as quite a surprise. We had climbed a hill and there was a barge apparently sailing along the meadows. We were stopped by a young Pennine Way walker who was looking for his four friends. He was their back-up for that day with a car. He had blisters, and talked about having two rest days. As he was a young man, all this made us feel very superior. (Mrs Davey – of Thornton in Craven – asked Herbert what he did about his job when he was away for so long. 'I'm retired,' he said. 'You must have retired very early,' was the flattering reply.)

Lunch today was not a happy experience. There was no-one else in the little craft shop and all round were notices which told us to 'remove muddy footwear', that it was not a 'look around' place, that 'all goods for sale could be seen in the window'. A large lady positioned herself in the doorway of what we assumed was the kitchen and glared at us as we were eating our sandwiches, as though she feared we would steal something if she did not keep watch. We were glad to leave. However, on visiting the public convenience wherein lay Gargrave's claim to sophistication, a lady said to me, 'I hear you're walking from Land's End to John o' Groats.' She must have been told by the man in the shop where we'd bought postcards.

It was a windy afternoon, but mainly dry. Soon after lunch we lost our way, as the previously excellent signposting let us down. Another walker seemed equally lost. We conferred together. He had no map or compass and decided to set off northwards, trusting entirely to his sense of direction. That wouldn't do for Herbert who studied his OS map and Wainwright alternately. Eventually our mapless optimist started beckoning furiously across two fields – he'd found the path. Good luck to him.

3.45 pm. We have arrived at Linden House Guest House in the picturesque village of Airton. The approach was along the river Aire, over a concrete bridge, then beside what had been a woollen mill, now converted into apartments. The centre of the village is one of the most attractive we've seen in Yorkshire, with old stone cottages surrounding the village green. Our guest house is further along the road and is a converted barn. We have a tiny room, but a marvellous view of sky and hills from the window. Downstairs is very attractive, with stone walls, raftered ceiling and a welcoming open fire. We were greeted by a young man in a white coat who produced tea and homemade cake. Then the friendly proprietress came to talk to us. There is an evening meal too which is a great blessing.

Day 53 – 13th June – Thursday

It has been pouring all night and looks like continuing (8.30 am) but last night the skies cleared and there was a glorious sunset.

The meal was amazing! The young chef (the proprietress's son) should be at the Savoy. It was a very rich meal and we couldn't cope with the sweet, but the whole thing was most unexpected in a little guest house. There was a creamy onion soup with light homemade bread rolls, and the main course was an intricate shell of light puff pastry stuffed with pieces of chicken breast in a fragrant lemon sauce. We were then offered a banana and brandy concoction adorned with cream which we reluctantly refused. The owner is far from sophisticated; she is a fat, jolly Yorkshire lady who enjoys listening to Herbert's Geordie stories. Chicken for the last three nights, Ponden Hall, Thornton in Craven and now Airton. Time for a change.

12.45 pm. Settle (halfway!). A pub with a log fire. Joan Robinson and her son, the chef, bade us a fond farewell and thanked us for staying with them. Ian, the son, told us there was a gentle climb then the road was downhill all the way. This was surely to encourage us. The climb lasted 3½ miles before the road levelled out and descended to Settle. There was a strong westerly wind blowing, with intermittent showers. But – it was a memorable walk, with magnificent views of the limestone hills all around us. The houses in Airton are different from the gritstone buildings we have seen during our days on the Pennine Way; the stone is no longer black, but a light creamy colour, and much less forbidding.

5.00 pm. Horton in Ribblesdale. A pretty awful afternoon's walk. The rain never let up at all. We walked on the road, as the footpath (the first of the Settle/Carlisle Way) was saturated, and the high ground in cloud. Arriving in Horton we had a pint mug of tea at the walkers' cafe, and met a group of Pennine Way walkers, one of whom was the young man with blisters we had met on the towpath yesterday. We signed the visitors book – previous signature 'Dave Smith L'End/John o' Groats'.

On arriving at our B & B, booked at the Information Centre in Settle, we were greeted by a young man who said he was a guest. He let us in and we saw that the tiny hall was full of boots and wet rucksacks. In the sitting room were five walkers. One couple had booked, the others were hoping to get fixed up here. The astonishing thing is that three of them, the couple who are booked and one young man, are all doing Land's End to John o' Groats (and we thought we were exceptional). One left Land's End on 21st April, the couple, who are Canadians, on the 25th.

9.45 pm. We have had a very sociable evening with the two Canadians. (In fact they are 'Brits' living in Canada.) They are being sponsored for Motor Neurone disease. The wife is very fed up with the poor weather. Let's hope it picks up tomorrow. The husband is carrying 27 lbs (compared with our 10/12 lbs): originally he had a video camera, battery charger etc., and cameras, one for slides and one for prints, but all of this equipment was discarded after 3 days.

Day 54 – 14th June – Friday   Gales and heavy rain all night. Our companions of last night set off very early to continue the Pennine Way to Hawes. We went on the road towards Dent as the path is waterlogged. Apart from the shortage of facilities – one loo for eight people – it was a pleasant B & B last night.

12 noon. Arrived in Ribbleshead sooner than expected. Should we try to go further? The choice lay between 4 miles or 11. Eventually we decided to be prudent. Eleven miles after lunch in bad weather is a bit risky. We will be having two short days, then a long one to Kirkby Stephen.

We had another inadequate cheese sandwich at the Ribbleshead pub – almost as poor as those in Settle yesterday which were the worst so far. But the proprietress of the pub is going on a world cruise on the Canberra in January so there has to be consideration for that. We have not attempted to leave the road since Settle, because everything is saturated. A walker came into the pub, black up to the top of his legs with peat. He was doing the Three Peaks. He had done one and determined never to do it again. Some of the Pennine Way walkers yesterday said they had been in worst ever conditions (mainly with the wind) so we are playing it safe. The railway is a disappointment and you still wonder why such an enormous undertaking is maintained for a few potty little 'Sprinters'. Maybe there will be steam tomorrow. There is a lot of activity on the Ribbleshead Viaduct so obviously BR is taking it seriously.

We talked to a sheep farmer after lunch. He was very depressed. The Government persuaded them all to produce more sheep, now the subsidies are being drastically reduced and they are being left holding the baby (lambs). If we heard of a farmer committing suicide we would know who it was. But he was beginning to dabble in shares.

3.15 pm. Arrived at our old friend 'The Sportsman'. We had wondered whether to attempt the 7 miles to The Moorcock (booked for tomorrow) but decided we couldn't manage it. That would have been 18 miles in total – too much for us.

9.00 pm. A cosy evening. There was a coal fire and a nice meal. Very few people in. A large lady sat all evening drinking beer while her two small children amused themselves as best they could. Two policemen were in early on (drinking coffee); they were investigating an armed robbery which had occurred in Sedbergh that afternoon.

Day 55 – 15th June – Saturday Clouds a bit higher, although still no sunshine. Short day today, only 7 miles.

1.00 pm. The Moorcock Inn, Garsdale. We have decided not to push on to Kirkby Stephen which is another 11 miles and it is pouring with rain. So we will have a long stay here. This place is not as attractive as The Sportsman but the landlord is welcoming and we have a reasonable room, although small. We have walked over the Coal Road which rises up to 1,600 ft. It was fine for the first hour or so then there was another torrential downpour. There were long distance views of the hills from the top, and even a glimpse of the Lakes.

9.30 pm. A half day! We spent the afternoon in bed and got up at seven for a meal, feeling much restored. We dined in a private dining room, not with the hoi polloi. The landlord's parents were at the next table. They are holidaying in a caravan and had called in for a meal. We chatted to them until bedtime. The same fat girl we saw in the Sportsman was in the bar, with children again in tow. She seems to go from pub to pub every evening.

Day 56 – 16th June – Sunday Everything looks sodden outside, but it is not raining at the moment.

Eleven miles to Kirkby Stephen on road. The hills are under cloud. A surprising day! We left the Moorcock at 10.00 am. Almost immediately heavy rain descended on us. It eased up a little, then by the time we reached the top of the 'long drag' it was coming down whole water. But our good fortune never fails us. There was a notice saying 'Aisgill Cottages B & B Craft shop, tea and coffee'. A cheerful lady gave us

Aisgill Summit

coffee and we chatted with her and her husband, telling them of some of our adventures. 'You should have stayed here last night,' she said. 'I'd have given you a meal.' Was she going to be in Kirkby Stephen tonight? asked Herbert. We'd love to come back with you. She wasn't, but rang a friend of hers and booked us in to a B & B at Kirkby Stephen, where we now are. We have a sitting room with a telly and a fire, and are getting a meal.

After our coffee break it was a good walk down Mallerstang from the source of the Eden. The rain stopped and we even had a glimpse of sunshine. The hills all around us were a picture, and the undulating road full of interest. It was after 2.00 pm before we found a pub and they had to be persuaded to give us anything: eventually they felt sorry for us. A pleasant footpath took us from Nateby to Kirkby Stephen. The people at this B & B have tried hard but haven't much idea. The meal was cooked by him. He would have benefited from cookery classes. She – a social worker – left before we did and he made our breakfast which, as it was toast and cereal only, was quite edible. One nice thing about this place was the card which said 'muddy boots welcome'. The host told us that sometimes the doorbell rang late at night and an exhausted Pennine Way walker literally fell into the house, and he would take off his boots and put him to bed – a kind man.

However, we are much in need of a change from B & Bs so will accept our friend Gordon's offer of a bed on Thursday.

Day 57 – 17th June – Monday

A late departure from Kirkby Stephen (10.30 am) as we did some shopping (replaced map case, travel soap). Wonder of wonders, the sun was shining for the first time for a fortnight so we bought a picnic lunch. We walked on minor roads through the Eden Valley with splendid views of the Pennines on our right (much better seen from the distance) and Wild Boar Fell behind us on our left. We came across a bright green corrugated iron hut which turned out to be Bleatarn Methodist Chapel (Herbert photographed it) and at a rise in the road a distant view of Blencathra appeared. The road was practically deserted except for occasional muck spreaders and only the plaintive cry of the curlew disturbed our peace, except when low flying jets blasted our eardrums from time to time. At one point we passed a row of dead crows strung up on a wire, presumably as a warning to their friends.

1.00 pm. We are now sitting by the roadside enjoying our pie and yoghurt; sadly the sun has gone in and there are ominous black clouds overhead. But it has been a sunny morning. Unwisely I suggested taking the Settle/Carlisle footpath as a change from the road, which we left when the signpost told us we were only four miles from Appleby. My goodness! This footpath, when we eventually found it, took us many more than four miles – firstly across fields, then along the river on a narrow, wet and muddy path for what seemed an eternity, then across more fields, still with no sign of Appleby. But all things, good and not so good, come to an end, and we finally reached the road. It was uphill again into the town, then down to the Information Centre. We were soon fixed up with bed and board, and an added bonus was a lift by our host up to the guest house. As by then (4.30 pm) it was raining cats and dogs and there was another half mile uphill, this was doubly welcome. We are once again bathed and changed and awaiting our supper. We hope it is better than last night.

9.20 pm. Yes, it was – lamb chops nicely cooked. We had a long talk with the only other guest who was also a walker. He had been in Scotland last week and said the weather was terrible! We spoke to Gordon who seems pleased we are going to stay with them for the night on Thursday. We rang Jane to discover we have had a *final* demand for our poll tax. We never got the first one. If not paid at once 'steps would be taken . . .'. Poor Jane has to deal with this. The garage has sold the SAAB. There's been a card from Mac from Tenerife. Helen is very miserable without Rob. Bedtime (a firm bed tonight).

Day 58 – 18th June – Tuesday Dull, looks like rain.

We found a Roman road which was very direct. Passed Kirkby Thore and left a note for Marjorie, then met Anne who had heard two hikers had been seen peering in her windows. Were they – er – not young? Oh yes! She knew at once who they were.

Another shortcut brought us to the Black Swan and sandwiches and coffee, where we are now sitting by a coal fire (and to think it is supposed to be mid-summer) chatting with a young couple. The husband is a member of the local mountain rescue team. He told us about the sophisticated medical equipment the rescue teams now have. Reluctantly we tore ourselves away from this refuge after waiting for two hours for the rain to stop. It was heavier than ever, but we plodded on and covered the remaining $3\frac{1}{2}$ miles to Langwathby in just over an hour.

The Good Samaritan. After 630 miles we have been offered a lift for the very first time. An old man on a tractor was sorry for the two drenched hikers. We thanked him profusely for his offer and explained why we couldn't accept it. So we just stood in the pouring rain while he told us his life history. He had left school at 13 and had never been anywhere really – 'd'you know what I mean' – never been in a train – 'd'you know what I mean'. I said he lived in a lovely place, and he thought very deeply, then said 'P'raps that's why'. There wasn't much life left for him, he said. He'd never had a day off work. He loved animals and thought it was their land not his – 'd'you know what I mean'. 'I'll p'raps read about you in the papers', he said. We had met a happy man.

4.30 pm. Langwathby, Cross Fell View. Drenched and cold, we rang the doorbell. No reply. We rang again and again no answer. We pushed the door open into a pretty hall. There was a note on the table: 'Make yourselves comfortable. You are in Room 2. Tea/coffee in lounge. Back soon.' We looked upstairs. There was obviously someone already in Room 2. Room 3 was also occupied. Room 1 had a bed but no sheets or blankets. So we returned to the lounge, which was warm and nicely furnished, and had tea and homemade biscuits. Soon after a gentleman came into the room. He had thought the note was for him so had taken over Room 2. He had also had a bath, using all the hot water. We were soon chatting like old friends. We waited for our hostess, who never came. Then another couple walked in. They obviously knew the setup and took some newspaper from a stand to stuff their boots (we'd put our wet rainwear and anoraks on the kitchen floor – a beautiful kitchen, but very cold). We waited and waited. The young couple reappeared, grumbling that there was no hot water which made our new friend, Terry, feel very uncomfortable. They were a withdrawn couple and seemed to resent our presence as they had already been there a week. At 6.30 pm our hostess still had not appeared so Herbert, Terry and I decided to go over to the pub for a meal hoping the bed situation would be sorted out in our absence. Unwashed and unchanged we went off in faith, leaving our wet gear in the kitchen, not knowing whether or not there would be a bed for us. We had a good meal and enjoyed Terry's company. He is a retired quantity surveyor, aged 65. His wife is a teacher but not fit enough for long distance walking. When we returned to our lodgings the situation was transformed. Our hostess, a young girl, had returned with her mother. They'd been to see the father who was in hospital. Our bed was made up. A coal fire was lit, more tea and biscuits produced. (The morose young couple remained in the pub.) We managed a hot bath at last (exotic bath with Jacuzzi) and went to bed. The bed was soft and lumpy and there was only one bathroom for everyone.

Day 59 – 19th June – Wednesday

We shared a table at breakfast with Terry and told him about Open University and painting. The other couple never spoke to us and left without a word. Cath, our hostess, said that they were staying for a fortnight and they were terrible.

We left at 10.00 am and walked a mile or so with Terry before parting company. Road and fields to the Druid's circle (Long Meg and her daughters). There were good views of Blencathra in sunshine. On roads again to Kirkoswald which boasts three pubs. We are in The Crown. The landlady has had a notice to quit by Whitbread which is sad for her as she doesn't want to leave. It seems there is no security in pub life.

3.15 pm. We have arrived at Lowfauld Farm. It is primitive and Herbert is getting weary of B & Bs and the labour of finding them. There is no room at Little Chef in Gretna. But we'll stick in and reach our goal somehow.

From the dining room window here there is a view of Blencathra and Little Mell Fell. We had a poor meal, but we are grateful for anything. We had a pot of tea with *one teabag*.

We rang Helen who was impressed by our progress (wish we were). Good news, Rob is coming home tomorrow. Bad news, he goes back to Australia after a week at home. Our landlady, the farmer's wife, is almost a bride (10 years married). She has a grown-up daughter and grandchildren from her first marriage who live in Greece; she used to live in Manchester and can't get used to country life and shop doors that don't open automatically.

Day 60 – 20th June – Thursday

A good night's sleep in spite of a soft bed. We awakened to clear skies and bright sunlight, and the sound of contented cows mooing gently outside our window.

2.50 pm. I am sitting in the taxi rank at Carlisle station. We are $1\frac{1}{2}$ hours early for our meeting with Gordon. After a cup of tea at a little cafe, Herbert has gone to the Tourist Information and I am guarding both rucksacks – we mustn't lose all our worldly goods.

It's been a beautiful morning and the walk from the farm to Carlisle was idyllic – that is, until we crossed over the M6 and started walking through this dreary town. The Pennines and Lakeland fells continued to be visible on either side of us as we continued along the Eden Valley – aptly named. We stopped at Cotehill to buy provisions for a picnic and were given £3 for CA, £2 from the shoplady and £1 from a customer – who reminded us, as if we didn't know only too well, that we still had a long way to go. A drunk, staggering along the footpath just before Carlisle, asked us how far it was to the next village (pub?) otherwise we've been alone. What has happened to the other Pennine Way walkers, we are wondering? Today for the first time for a week we have been able to see the tops. Perhaps summer has come at last.

REST Day – 21st June – Friday – Midsummer day It is raining and foggy, yesterday was a 'one off'.

We had a peaceful sunny drive to Gosforth yesterday, and very warm welcome from Gordon and June. We were given tea, had a bath, washed our hair, had a wonderful meal, and chatted until bedtime. This morning we have made up a parcel for Jane and I made use of June's washing machine. Herbert had his hair cut by a 'dolly bird' at the local hairdressers.

We booked up the next few nights and the CA rep. is going to help us with accommodation on the next stretch if things get too difficult. Now – 1.00 pm – we are in the train on our way back to Carlisle. June has made us a picnic lunch so we'll enjoy the ride in spite of the gloom and fog.

4.30 pm. In yet another B & B, this time in Carlisle. This one is a great improvement on the farm where we stayed two nights ago, but not to compare with our good friends' hospitality of last night. Various disasters have occurred since the last entry. Watching a video of Carlisle's history in the Tourist Office Herbert suddenly realised he'd left his map case, with map and measuring pencil, in the train. We replaced what we could, then asked the station to try to find the missing objects. Second disaster – the man in the shop said that next week the A74 – our only route to Glasgow – will be a motorway and thus barred to walkers. There sure are problems in walking through the British Isles. There is one blessing, however. This B & B has a telly in our room so Herbert can watch the Test Match. (Poor meal at the County Hotel.)

* * *

Thoughts of Scotland

You may feel that Scotland gets a bad press in the ensuing pages. They have a problem with the weather of course, but that does not seem to deter the visitors; they still pour in in their droves, so many in foreign registered cars that it is a wonder we still have a balance of payments deficit. The real shock comes when you cross the border and all of a sudden you discover that you are without places to eat and drink. It is a traumatic experience, not exclusively ours we should add, but the experience of the majority of travellers we meet. The hardened tourists treat it as something of a joke, one of those national peculiarities that makes the life of the tourist so interesting. 'Scotland?' they say. 'Oh yes! no tea.' England offers you a constant succession of public houses with the opportunity not only of liquid refreshment but also the cheese or ham sandwich to sustain you in the middle of the day. (Do you know that the price of a sandwich varies between 85p and £1.90? The cheaper ones are obtainable in those pubs which are in sight of other pubs.) In Scotland you search the highways and by-ways in vain. When one does appear you are sure it is a mirage. There must be a logical explanation for this state of affairs, but to the uninitiated it is very much a puzzlement. Why, when Scotland is no longer industrialised but more and more dependent upon its faithful tourists, can it not offer them tea? When there is so much unemployment why doesn't somebody open a tea shop? If anyone were to set up a chain of refreshment establishments his name would be Paul Getty in next to no time. But every cloud has a silver lining. The local inhabitants – bless their hearts! – seem aware of the situation, and we did receive frequent invitations to drink tea along the road. And that is a heart-warming experience, because one of the greatest acts of charity is to offer a cup of tea to a thirsty walker.

The other problem in Scotland is the West Highland Way. Theoretically you are free to roam anywhere you want in Scotland, which is perhaps the reason for the lack of long distance footpaths – they are not strictly necessary. But it does mean that enthusiastic walkers in their thousands descend on the West Highland and churn up the footpath and fill what local establishments there are. We read in the West Highland Way newsheet that erosion is becoming a serious problem (and we can confirm that). There have been attempts to patch up some of the worst places (and some heroic voluntary work to rebuild the culverts on a section of General Wade's road), but there seems no hope of doing anything to that really hazardous track along the bonny, bonny banks of Loch Lomond – unless a helicopter is used. The only suggestion that the West Highland Way newsheet had to offer to relieve the rate of deterioration was that walkers should try one of the other two long distance footpaths – not a very positive solution to the problem. One further niggle before we leave the West Highland. In spite of the 'Walkers are Welcome' campaign instituted by the Scottish Tourist Board – and hundreds of little blue stickers appeared wherever there was food and accommodation to reassure us of that fact – there were places when we had the distinct impression that we were not; rather that we were a blooming nuisance. So walkers, if you ever come across that blue circle expressing the promise 'walkers welcome', treat it with reserve; there is a chance that it might not be true.

How grateful we were in Scotland to the bridge builders! From Inverness onwards we were carried across the great inlets of the sea on their magic carpets, and escaped dozens of extra miles tramping thanks to them. No doubt the motorists are grateful as well – presumably these wonders of modern engineering were produced for the benefit of the tourist on wheels – but it is difficult to express the walkers' sense of appreciation of these splendid short cuts.

* * *

Day 61 – 22nd June – Saturday

We're off to Scotland at last. It is a fine morning, but still overcast. A CA man contacted us about a radio phone-in: he was very little help, so we'll forget it. The route to Glasgow is difficult. We'll start off on the A74 and see how far we get.

1.20 pm. Metal Bridge Inn on the A74. We left Carlisle at 10.00 am. The road took us over a beautiful park, colourful and with many graceful weeping willows. Thereafter it was a long tedious haul to get out of the city. We managed to avoid a stretch of the A74 by taking a long detour along minor roads. Heavy showers alternated with some sunny periods, but the weather is improving.

3.00 pm. We have crossed the border into Scotland – a milestone on our journey. We were greeted by a piper wearing a kilt, and playing traditional Scottish tunes at the Tollhouse. We took his photograph and he gave us 50p for CA. Most people pay him for his entertainment. We booked in at our B & B. It's an uninspiring place, full of tiny rooms with doors that open outwards like prison cells. But it is full.

Gretna Green is very 'trippery'. We wandered up to the Old Smithy where there were crowds, coaches, shops full of tourist rubbish, but it was by then a sunny afternoon which makes such a difference to life. Our walk along the dreaded A74 wasn't too awful as we could use the grass verge. It is true that it is to be upgraded into a motorway but not for a couple of years so we'll be all right.

9.20 pm. A most surprising evening. When we arrived in Gretna we dumped our haversacks, then went to see what were the prospects for a meal. There were two horrid cafeterias: one closed early but the other had an upstairs restaurant. The owner advised us to book a meal as it was popular. This turned out to be a revelation. The upstairs was in a different class altogether from the plastic place downstairs. It was nicely furnished and carpeted, and as soon as we arrived we were shown to a table for two by the window with an expansive view over the border hills. It was a fine evening and there were magnificent cloud effects. A waitress told us to go through an archway where we would be served. There was an absolute feast awaiting us. We were invited to choose from 6–8 different starters, each equally delicious. We both had a piece of juicy melon. There was a whole roast turkey, a huge piece of roast ham, a leg of lamb and a joint of beef. We were told to have a slice of each (we did). There were perfect yorkshire puds, vegetables, stuffings, three different gravies and various trimmings. Everything was expertly cooked and presented. The chef told us to come back for more if still hungry. To crown it all there was a choice of about a dozen homemade sweets and very good coffee. It cost less than the miserable meal we had in Carlisle. We never know what is going to happen next on this journey.

Day 62 – 23rd June – Sunday

A glamorous guest in a dressing gown greeted us with 'Another nasty morning'. We were disturbed during the night by a pile-driver, relentlessly pounding away at the A74, busy turning it into a motorway, but we shut the window which helped a bit. Very good bed.

Breakfasts in most B & Bs are standard. Bacon/egg/sausage/tomato (sometimes tinned), white sliced bread as toast, cereals – cornflakes, weetabix (occasionally a more interesting muesli), plastic butter and marmalade and weak tea. As we never eat anything cooked, our breakfasts are less than interesting. Yet people seem to like them. This place, which advertises central heating (not turned on even though it is very cold), is full-up. Most of the rooms have a telly and in this one the ever-present square box is perched beneath the ceiling. To watch it you must lie flat on your back with your eyes fixed heavenward which is very uncomfortable. This B & B is purely a tourist processing factory. Take 'em in, provide the minimum necessities and push 'em out as soon as possible. It is so different from the majority of the places we stayed in earlier on.

Today began dismally, with dark heavy clouds and drizzling rain. It has ended with brilliant sunshine. So we must never despair. We managed to keep off the A74 for most of the day as the old road runs more or less parallel with it. The landscape seemed dull and uninteresting, but that may have been due to the weather. We passed through some hamlets which were poor little places, although one cottage had the imaginative name of 'Two Hoots' with the picture of an owl above it. We'd passed one church – at Kirkpatrick – just at the right time for the morning service only to find it was the wrong Sunday in the month. As we went further on lonely roads there was less chance of any lunch; we returned to the A74 and found a pub which was open in spite of it being in Scotland and on the Sabbath. We had our usual sandwiches and cider, and before we knew what was happening we were both tipsy. It was the most powerful cider we had ever tasted. So we stayed a while to let the effects calm down. When we told the landlord, he just smiled and said it would put a spring in our step. It certainly drove the clouds away as the day was transformed by the time we left. There followed another stint on the A74 until we reached the birthplace of Thomas Carlyle – Ecclefechan – where we found accommodation. This B & B is an improvement on last night as far as space is concerned as we have a huge room. Alas no PFs or even a washbasin in our room. There is only one 'facility' to be shared among all the guests. So far we don't know how many there are. We are eating in tonight which is nice, but we do not expect the meal to come up to last night's standard. We are making progress and will be in Glasgow by the weekend.

Day 63 – 24th June – Monday

After a sunny afternoon yesterday it is again dull, but there is a fairly cheerful forecast.

We had a reasonable meal here with Mrs Martin, then spent the evening chatting with a couple from Bromley who seemed fascinated by our experiences. They had just been to John o' Groats and were very impressed by northern Scotland.

Sitting at the breakfast table we are watching a lady across the road feeding her pet duck, which appears to be a lame one.

Ecclefechan is a quaint little village of only one street. We are staying opposite the house where Thomas Carlyle was born, but it doesn't appear to have the tourist pull of Lovers' Leap in Gretna.

4.30 pm. A haven of rest after a long, hard day. We left Ecclefechan at 10 o'clock. Our landlady gave us £5 for Christian Aid in spite of the fact that her charges were the lowest yet – £26 for dinner, bed and breakfast. She had lived in Ghana for some years and was therefore very interested in the African Famine Appeal.

We began our walk today with a couple of hours on the A74 until we reached Lockerbie. Herbert went to the station to see if the map case had turned up (it hadn't), then back on our old friend (?) after this diversion. Lockerbie is a clean tidy town, bigger than we had imagined, and no sign of the damage caused by the bombed jet. We were then fortunate to find a series of minor roads. We came to a small village and had hopeful thoughts of lunch. There was nothing. We had a Mars bar and an apple between us. Also drank some water from an outside tap, and continued on in the hope there would be a teashop in the next village. Nothing again. Even the post office had disappeared. While we were eating our Mars bar a man in a postal van emptied the letter box on the village green – contents, one letter. We decided to push on until we reached the farm where we had booked a room. On the telephone Herbert had enquired about an evening meal. No, was the reply, but there's a pub only five miles down the road. However, on hearing we were walking they agreed, very cheerfully, to feed us.

We had no great expectations after some of our previous experiences of farms, and we have been most pleasantly surprised. The young farmer and his wife were just about to go out to collect their children from school, but nevertheless greeted us with great enthusiasm. When they heard we had not eaten all day they told us to make ourselves a sandwich. They showed us our room which is the prettiest we have had for ages. We are surrounded by fields and there is absolute peace and quiet. There is a telly, which is not on the ceiling, a washbasin, plenty of space, and it is all beautifully furnished and decorated. We are very happy – 13 miles today.

8.45 pm. We have had a lovely meal. This is a friendly family who are very anxious to please us. A young Australian couple are also staying and we listened in astonishment to the description of their trip which is a three-month one, like ours. The difference is that we are spending the time walking through one country, whereas they have been all over the British Isles and Europe, and intend to return (to Adelaide) via Thailand and Bangkok. They have been saving up for two years for this holiday. Neither of them has been to Europe before so they are very excited. The trouble, they told us, was that when taken on guided tours round the various cities they were so busy writing down the information they were given they had not time to look at the places they were visiting. Our hostess is a Yorkshire lady who loves living in Scotland. In this remote area the people really care for each other, she said. One night they had some trouble with their dairy machinery; someone saw the light on and came to see what was wrong. Could they help? The locals make their own entertainment, often gathering in one of the farms and playing instruments like the good old days.

Day 64 – 25th June – Tuesday

A good firm bed and we slept well in this peaceful place. This morning it is pouring with rain again. Where, oh where, is the summer?

6.00 pm. This has not been a happy day. The weather has been less than kind, and we have been pounding away on a monotonously straight road all day. Low cloud prevented us from seeing what was probably a good view, but the young bullocks were, as always, pleased to see us. Resting at Beattock summit, 1,069 ft, sitting on the ground in a lay-by (no seats in Scotland either) what should we see but the royal train. We had been walking alongside the main Glasgow–Euston line all morning. We waved to them. Eventually – at 1.00 pm – we arrived in the long awaited 'town' of Beattock. It consisted of one street of dreary little houses, one pub which was closed, and a very smelly little cafe. We met a young Swiss couple coming out of this establishment saying it was full of smoke. We decided to go in out of the cold, but quickly retreated. It wasn't smoke, but an overwhelming smell of cooking oil. We went to the little shop at the back of the cafe and bought some milk and cheese etc. and sat outside on a very shabby picnic seat beside the Swiss couple. We started to talk to them (in my very bad German). 'Why are you walking here when you have the Swiss mountains?' we enquired. 'Too difficult, too expensive, you need a guide', was the reply. They were doing the Southern Upland Way which crosses Scotland from west to east. They wished us luck. We were just leaving when we were startled by a huge shape flying over our heads – it was a peacock in full flight.

We continued and soon reached Moffat. Now there's a place! Beautifully laid out, expensive looking houses, colourful park. There are lots of B & Bs which encouraged us. We went to the Tourist Office, passed the park (which we learned later, was responsible for Moffat winning the 'Scotland in Bloom Award') and booked in at *very* superior accommodation which is more like a hotel. It is a wonderful old house, probably built about the turn of the century, like the one in Buxton. We were at a low point when we arrived, but a spacious room and an excellent meal of Scotch broth, salmon and Gallic pudding, as well as a good night's sleep, have restored our confidence. We were talking to an elderly couple after dinner and the husband said sweetly, 'I wish we could do something to help you' – but evidently didn't think of the obvious – a donation.

Day 65 – 26th June – Wednesday A better morning, cloudy but brighter, and no rain (yet).

Apparently the weathermen are more optimistic. This is going to be a difficult stretch for accommodation – we'll try the Tourist Board again before we leave Moffat. Herbert spoke to Jane last night. She thought we were making good progress. She will send the next parcel to the Christian Aid office in Glasgow.

5.45 pm. Crawford. Once more we are bathed, changed and awaiting a meal. We have had a most interesting day. We left Hartfell House with great reluctance. It was a place reminiscent of the gracious past. We heard it had belonged to the local doctor. Our room was an attic on the top floor, but large and very attractive, with fine old furniture. But we had to leave it, after a real Scottish breakfast of porridge and oatcakes. We have happy memories of our stay in Moffat.

The Tourist Board fixed us up with a B & B here in Crawford which we learned was 14 miles from Moffat; there was nothing nearer.

Today's walk began with a steep climb out of the town. There were hills all round us and the sunshine was a bonus. We both felt refreshed after our good night and were going well. Suddenly in front of us a gentleman got out of his car. He approached and asked if he could give us a lift as there was a long climb ahead. We thanked him and explained why we could not accept his kind offer. He immediately put his hand in his pocket and gave us a pound. We chatted to him for a while and discovered that he was a retired GP living in Moffat. He reminded us very much of Dr Cameron of Dr Finlay's Casebook. After we parted – but not before he'd told us his name was Hugh Sinclair and that we would be very welcome at his home at any time – we continued uphill among Forestry Commission fir trees until we heard, far below, the roar of the A74 once again. There is nothing to eat in Scotland, we have realised through bitter experience (oh! for those English pubs), so just before meeting the busy road at Greenhead Stairs we ate what we had – some sandwiches left over from yesterday, half an apple and drank some water out of our bottle. Then it was on to the A74 for the rest of the day. There were various possible deviations but we have made up our minds to get to Glasgow as fast as possible.

We made good progress (3 mph) until we arrived at some major roadworks about which warning notices had been appearing for some time. Do you remember that the A74 was being upgraded to a motorway? We were stuck! It was too dangerous to follow the diverted traffic as there was no grass verge to walk on, and the engineers were making huge holes in the old road. What was to be done? We approached three young men in hard hats for advice. We explained our predicament. They piled us and our rucksacks into one of their cars and drove us through the danger zone. Our first, and last, lift. It was either cheating or losing our lives, so we felt it was justified. We still had some roadworks to negotiate (one of our young rescuers turned up again and apologised for dropping us too soon) but we were buoyed up with the prospect of tea, as a notice recently passed, announced 'services ½ mile, meals served all day'. We got nearer and nearer, 200 yards, 100 yards, each notice increasingly whetting our appetites. The final notice said 'WELCOME'. We turned a corner and saw a tatty looking pre-fab type of construction, with a large notice on the door saying 'CLOSED'. We went disconsolately into a little shop attached to the nearby garage and asked pathetically if they had any tea. The girl behind the counter pointed to a machine which dispensed various liquids. There was no tea, only mushroom soup. We bought fruit juice, then had an amusing conversation with two Scotsmen who couldn't understand why anyone should want to hike along the A74. 'That's no' a holiday,' said one. 'Give me Majorca.' He could be right. A mile further on we came to the junction to Crawford, and eventually to our B & B. It was not to compare with the magnificence of last night, but it is clean and adequate.

Evelyn, our hostess, has just gone to make us some coffee. She has been talking to us all the evening. Her husband is a lorry driver, and presumably away. She told us she, like Herbert, is a cancer survivor. We mentioned Dr Sinclair and she said he was her doctor when she lived in Moffat. He was suffering from Alzheimer's disease – the early stages – which is very sad. She also knew the people who used to live in Hartfell House when it was a private house. We eventually got away from the flow of conversation at 10 o'clock. Facilities are pretty awful. We are in a downstairs bedroom. The bathroom and only washbasin and loo are upstairs, also the cistern takes about 20 minutes to refill which delays matters, and there are other guests. But we had a good homecooked meal. Also tea and cake when we arrived, and coffee and more cake later in the evening. But for us adequate toilets and washbasins are the top priority.

Day 66 – 27th June – Thursday Today is dull again, but we hope it will get out as it did yesterday.

7.00 pm. What a day! Evelyn made us a sandwich so that we wouldn't starve in this barren land. After posting off maps and diaries to Jane we set off along the back road to the north as we had had quite enough of the A74 for a while. The clouds were low but it stayed dry and we walked among bare hillsides rather similar to the Lakes. After a short rest by a river we were once again on an A road, but this one was quieter. At about 1.20 pm we reached a perfect picnic place, again by a river. It was warm and we both went to sleep. Refreshed, we continued along a quiet road towards the A72 on our way to Glasgow. As we reached this junction a car approached us, stopped, and a man got out and walked towards us. Herbert was just saying to himself that he looked just like Tom Bennett, when we both realised it was Tom Bennett. He had come all the way from Sunderland to meet us. The story gradually unfolded. Tom had intended to come and see us round about Carlisle but after returning from holiday he had spoken to Jane and discovered we were a long way past there. Jane had rung him back on Tuesday to say that we were at Moffat and hoped to be in Crawford the next night. Tom had set out in faith (and great devotion) and by a happy chance had called in the Tourist Information at the Little Chef at Abington. He was looking for two walkers called Witherington and was told that two people of that name had been at a B & B in Crawford. He rang Evelyn who told him they were on the way to Symington. Tom set off along the A73, left the car, walked 20 minutes but with no success. He went back to the car, drove towards the B-road and was about to turn down it when he saw us. It was, yet again, a miracle. We sat in his car – a new one – for an hour or so, drank his coffee and heard the wonderful news that Herbert had won a Highly Commended at the Laing for the painting of the wreck, which also had been sold. It was all too much. Tom drove his car to Symington. We walked, without haversacks – and he came to meet us. We all walked together to Symington where we said goodbye, but not until he had given us an apple and three chocolate biscuits. Goodbye to a wonderful act of friendship.

Then we walked into Symington and booked in at the only accommodation – a posh hotel. This is a treat after some of the B & Bs we have been in. We have a gorgeous room with all mod cons. We have had salmon en croûte and a glass of wine, so we are feeling very happy. But my evening blouse has split under the arm which is a disaster. We had a long talk with Rob. He is going to tell the Bank he cannot go back to Australia. We rang Carr House and gave the room number to Keith. 'Oh it's like that, is it?' was his comment. Gillian is very happy in France; the rest of the family are busy doing all her jobs.

A friend rang Jane. 'I don't want to worry Herbert, but he'll find accommodation very difficult in Scotland.' She'd also written to me, 'Be warned, the midges are terrible in

Scotland.' And Will promised us our spines would crumble.

If we listened to all this we'd give up today.

Day 67 – 28th June – Friday Tinto Hotel, Symington. Daily weather report, dull, dry.

It was a fun breakfast at our luxury hotel. I had fresh grapefruit for once. Then we both ordered Ayrshire ham and cheese. There arrived for each of us three large slices of ham and some delicious Scottish cheddar cheese. We waited until the waitresses, who were all dressed in white shirts and tartan kilts, had left the dining room, then Herbert wrapped some of the ham and cheese in his serviette and stuffed it under his sweater. Fortunately we were the last people down to breakfast so no-one observed the felony.

We were late in leaving as we didn't really want to part from our beautiful room, but all good things come to an end, and at 10.30 am we were on the road once more. For some of the time we were able to use attractive minor roads but after a couple of hours were back on the 'A'. We crossed the Clyde on the old Kirkfield Bridge built in 1773. Looking over we saw a man knee deep in the water, fishing. I wonder if he caught any salmon. As usual we had passed nothing remotely like a pub, cafe or anything at all offering food, so at halfpast one we found a spot slightly off the busy road and unwrapped our ham and cheese; this, together with some biscuits we'd taken from our hotel room and Tom's chocolate biscuits and apple, made a good lunch. And we had filled our bottle with water. Goodness knows where travellers in

Kirkfield Bridge

Scotland are supposed to eat. A number of hotels seem to be derelict, and even the private houses are, for the most part, run down and shabby, although people take a great pride in their gardens. The lawns are immaculate.

After our free lunch we continued along the main road into Lanark, and by this time there was a pavement which saved us from the ever present danger of ending up like the many squashed rabbits we have seen by the roadside. The Tourist Office was as helpful as everywhere else and booked us into a B & B by the river. We would have liked to go further to shorten tomorrow's walk but nothing was found the few miles further we had hoped to go. Why anyone wants to come to Lanark is a mystery. It is a very uninteresting place. We asked the lady in the Tourist Office about teashops and she said there was a very nice family-run cafe just down the road called 'The Original Teapot'. We went in to this with high hopes, to be greeted by a smelly, smoky atmosphere (it is surprising how many people smoke in Scotland), paper tablecloths, and on the only vacant table a dirty dishcloth was lying. We should have walked out, but we ordered a pot of tea (90p) which was virtually undrinkable. We left hurriedly and started the steep descent to the river where we found our B & B. It is not the Tinto of last night of course, but we have a big airy room, and have been promised mince steak for supper by our glamorous young hostess. She also made us some decent tea which took away the taste of the other. We have windows at both ends of our room. The back window looks down to the river and to the fields and hills beyond. There is a big caravan site on the opposite river bank, but if you ignore that it is a good view. The sitting room where we had tea is elaborately and expensively furnished, and there is a smart bathroom (mahogany toilet seat and gold taps). We have found this kind of luxury in many of our B & Bs, BUT – no washbasin in our bedroom.

Again only one bathroom with loo and washbasin which we find inconvenient.

Day 68 – 29th June – Saturday First day of summer. It has come at last. We have a wonderful sunny morning.

There is a startling sight across the river today – banks of trees on the hillside which rises in different shades of green up to a gap in the wall on the skyline.

5.30 pm. We are comfortably settled in Hamilton's Travel Lodge on the M74. It has been a tiring day, probably because we have been on a busy road all the time. But it has been a scenic route – the Clyde Valley Tourist Route – which follows the river all the way. After an hour's walking during which we had passed village after village without a shop, we found one which had these in abundance, as well as cafes and restaurants. We bought something for a picnic, and continued along the A8. There was a lot of traffic but no lorries, and we enjoyed the views over the Clyde Valley. Just after buying our lunch we came across an exotic garden centre with an attractive coffee shop – so we sat in the sunshine among the flowers, drank coffee and ate a gooey chocolate thing. After resting our feet for half an hour we set off once more along the valley road. The sun gradually lost the argument with the clouds but there was a soft breeze blowing so it was good walking weather. The Clyde Valley must be the garden of Scotland. There are orchards, fruit farms (strawberry picking has started), fields of vegetables and a large number of greenhouses. About one o'clock we began looking for a quiet spot off the road for our picnic but there didn't seem anywhere suitable, just a lot of houses at that point. In one front garden a gentleman was busy cutting the grass. We stopped to admire his tidy garden. He smiled and asked us if we would like a cup of tea. Wouldn't we just! We went into the house and sat in his sun lounge to eat our picnic in comfort. Our kind Scotsman made us tea and insisted on giving us a banana each. Indeed he would have even have given us a bed if we had needed it. He had a sad story to tell us. His wife was in hospital with a deteriorating kidney condition. His father had recently died (aged 100) and Alex Ritchie – our benefactor's name – showed us a picture of a fine old gentleman in a kilt, also a telegram from the Queen. The old man had never been ill, but suddenly had trouble with his gullet, was operated on and died. Alex's son had emigrated to Australia, which had broken his mother's heart as the boy had never been back and the parents would not fly. The house was built by Alex's father and the garden went down to the river. The fishing rights of the stretch covering the garden belonged to the owner of the house which we thought very romantic. After an hour of this hospitality we felt we must resume our task: we shook him warmly by the hand, while he tried to persuade us to take with us a lettuce from his greenhouse. What great kindness we continually receive!

It seemed a long way to Hamilton, and when we got there it was a dirty crowded place which we were anxious to get out of. Herbert rang up the Travel Lodge and found there was a room for us. Like all Travel Lodges, the room and facilities are excellent, but the food – at the cafeteria beside the Lodge – is dreadful. We had very greasy bacon, sausage and egg. Tomorrow we must have an early start as we are due in Glasgow at 2.00 pm and we have ten miles to walk.

Day 69 – 30th June – Sunday

At last we have made it to Glasgow, and have just completed the worst day of our journey. We had a disgracefully expensive and totally inadequate breakfast at the Travel Lodge. Herbert told them they should all be put in prison for robbery. The man in charge apologised and said they were trying to upgrade the restaurant, and in the meantime many of the overnight residents went to Marks and Spencers for their breakfast. We got a taxi back to Hamilton shopping centre from where we had deviated to the Lodge, and apart from a brief interlude have been in built-up areas all day. The usual problem in towns – toilet facilities, or lack thereof – was a cause for concern. We were horrified at the dirt and shabbiness of the buildings, but we have been told that this part of the walk is a necessary discipline. We spoke to an elderly road sweeper who was clearing up the weekend debris. A telephone kiosk was completely smashed, and there was broken glass everywhere. The old man said he had a never-ending job. He also told us things were very hard in Scotland – no real money, just credit.

After many dull and weary miles of slums, enlivened only briefly by a cheerful and colourful Orange Day procession, we came across a shopping centre – Rutherglen – which seemed a little better, and actually had some pubs. Alas! it was only 12 o'clock and they all opened at 12.30 pm. We trudged on, telling ourselves that this walk was the experience of a lifetime. We eventually found one hostelry which was open, but there was nothing to eat. At least we could have a drink and make use of the facilities. Just before 2 o'clock we arrived at the home of the Christian Aid representative where we had been promised a bed. They had very kindly prepared a cold lunch for us but were anxious to go out. Every Sunday they visited the gentleman's mother-in-law in Edinburgh. They said they would probably be very late so we may not see them until breakfast time.

After our lunch we both collapsed into bed and slept for a couple of hours. We went to church at six: the vicar donated £10 to Christian Aid.

1st July – Monday Raining.

After mutual photograph taking, Tony Ashcroft – our host – drove us to the Burrell Museum where there is a fascinating collection of objet d'art of all kinds, tapestries, paintings, glass and porcelain, furniture, sculpture from many parts of the world and from many different periods of history, all donated to the city by a wealthy shipowner. After a couple of hours which included a free guided tour, it was still raining heavily, so heavily that the roof was leaking; through the great glass walls we could see plainly what was waiting for us when we left. We decided we would have some lunch and then plough on – although we had nowhere to sleep. At this point we were informed by a disembodied voice over the loudspeaker that the restaurant was closed until further notice. This dire warning, repeated at frequent intervals, eventually penetrated even our bemused minds. Herbert bought a postcard of a Degas painting and started writing it to Helen. I read what he had written and said, 'You can't send that: it is too depressing.' He looked up with despair in his eyes and said in a weak voice, 'You know I can't go on, don't you'. I went to the public telephone at the entrance, rang Peggie and told her we were coming home.

9th July – Tuesday

We have arrived in Milngavie (pronounced 'Mullguy') refreshed and ready to renew the battle. In the train from Glasgow we had talked over the crisis and decided to take a rest and try again. We remained in our own home concealed from the outside world for a week with dear Peggie caring for us. We managed to escape detection, thanks to her ingenuity. The last thing we wanted was for the news to get around that we had given up. We slept long hours; we watched Wimbledon and the Test Match; Herbert painted; and Peggie looked after us. A week later a taxi came for us at 11.00 am. We caught the Edinburgh Intercity at 11.30 am, then the Glasgow connection. We are now at the first stage of the West Highland Way.

We have a pleasant B & B but no evening meal so we went, on a sunny, windy evening, to a Berni Inn. We are hoping this good weather will continue when we recommence our pilgrimage tomorrow. (Great shock to learn yesterday of the death of that dear soul Kendal Baker. We sent flowers to Joyce by Interflora.) Family news, Jane, Gillian and David have flown to California today for a walking holiday. Milngavie is a leafy, pleasant place, on the edge of the Campsie Hills. The open vistas are a welcome change from Glasgow's concrete jungle. Again, as we have noticed during our walk through southern Scotland, the gardens are all carefully tended but, apart from our B & B – which is a two-storeyed semi – the houses are mainly bungalows, with occasional windows in the roof. It seems to make no difference whether they are modern brick-built houses or old stone ones – they are all very small and single-storeyed. It must be quite difficult to bring up a family in such tiny houses. Glasgow –

by contrast, at least in the centre – is composed of tenement blocks four or five storeys high. There were six separate households living in the building where we stayed. Each family had to use the same entrance – an old-fashioned green-tiled corridor which led to the individual front doors.

Day 70 – 10th July – Wednesday

We are on the road again. At two minutes past nine we began the West Highland Way and have walked for approximately six hours. The weather is hot and sticky, but no sun. The flies are troubling us for the first time. No midges yet, but we have been promised them on Rannoch Moor. We have met a few walkers including four young boys. The way from Milngavie began with a forest path, then a disused railway line. There were views of the Campsie Hills on our left. Our hostess had provided us with a packed lunch – free of charge – but for once we came across a pub, so we bought a drink and sat outside to eat our sandwiches.

Drymen – our stop for tonight – is a pretty village, the best we have seen so far in Scotland. Our B & B is disappointing however. The room is tiny and the bed very soft, which is bad for walkers. There is one bath, washbasin and loo and this is downstairs, but at least no-one else uses it. The other guests all have their own PFs.

We have just come in from the self-styled 'oldest pub in Scotland'. I rather doubt that, but it was pleasant with blue velvet chairs and a colourful tartan carpet. Interestingly there has been a change for the better since we last walked the West Highland Way. The numerous stiles along the path have been replaced with very clever gadgets which open as you meet them and close automatically behind you. Much better than heaving yourself and your baggage over the high stiles that used to litter the West Highland.

Day 71 – 11th July – Thursday We have reached Loch Lomond.

It is pouring with rain. We are in a coffee house waiting for it to stop, and are wondering whether we will be here for the night. We became very attached to our hosts of last night (as we so often do). The wife is Scottish; the husband, who made the breakfast, is Italian. All the guests sat together at a big table and enjoyed melon, fresh grapefruit, well cooked bacon, orange juice, toast and marmalade. Mr and Mrs Bolzicco were very kind to us. They gave us £5 for Christian Aid, and also telephoned all over the place for accommodation for two walkers, Dutch and Austrian. We think we had the cheapest room as the CA rep. who booked it up probably wanted to save us money. We certainly had a happy stay. Mr Bolzicco made us tea when we arrived and again in the evening. A father and son who had stayed there when they began the Way called in on their way home to say how much they had enjoyed the hospitality they had received.

This morning we have cut out the hill specified on the Way and have walked down the road to Balmaha, passing some attractive houses and a big nursery. It was a leafy road, but there were no views owing to the low cloud. We will be alongside the loch for the next two days, but this afternoon our walk is all through forest.

3.00 pm. We have cut our losses. Starting on the Way after our coffee break we climbed steeply through sodden bracken to reach a marvellous viewpoint from where we could see over the loch. On a fine day it would have been breathtaking – even today in the rain with the clouds right down it was spectacular. We then descended to the lochside, but as the torrent continued we reluctantly returned to the road and continued on this until we reached Rowardennan. The rain was remorseless, and finding no other shelter we eventually ate our cheese and apple in a telephone box which appeared miraculously in this lonely area. At least it was dry.

Now we are bathed, dried out and have had tea, so life is rosy again.

Lunch

Day 72 – 12th July – Friday Rain, rain, rain!

We left Rowardennan in a downpour which continued until about 4.00 pm. It has been a very rough day, as we were on the footpath beside the loch which became muddier and more slippery as the day – and the rain – continued. We met two German schoolboys who were camping, poor things. We reached Inversnaid soon after 1.00 pm where there is a very high-class hotel. All the poor, sodden walkers piled in through the back door and divested themselves of their outer clothing. We had soup – not hot – and shared our sandwiches with the boys. Then we resumed our battle with the mud and rain. At long last rescue came in the shape of a cheerful ferryman who answered our signal (two large balloons hoisted high up on a pole). He came across the loch in a little red boat and brought us, together with the Germans and three Dutch boys, over the loch to Ardlui and, mercifully, a road which was a great improvement on the muddy footpath. By then the sun had come out so the last couple of miles were more pleasant than the previous ones.

We have done 13 miles today, and eight hours walking – not exactly a record speed.

We are again at Inverarnan and it is as dirty and shabby as

it was the last time we stayed here. But it is very *popular*. The bar is packed. We are in the bridal suite, but the bride must have used it about 300 years ago. We were told soon after we were here previously that the hotel was under new management. There are no visible signs of this, rather the general air of shabbiness and neglect has been re-emphasised. We wonder how such an establishment meets the hygiene regulations and the attentions of the Tourist Board, or indeed why anyone comes into the place. Yet they pour in in their hundreds. All the rickety chairs and broken tables are occupied. The food – which was remarkably appetising – comes flowing out of the bowels of the inn (not a very well chosen phrase) and people of all sorts from long-haired campers and cigar-smoking foreigners to highly respectable citizens come in in a constant procession. One elegant lady said to us, 'I hear you are staying here.' 'Yes.' 'Have you stayed here before?' 'Yes.' 'How wonderful.' I thought of taking her up to the attic where we have been 'stalled', but the effort would have been too much. So we are left to wonder at the magnetic effect of 'character', and how we are going to survive the night without the bed collapsing. I would like to describe it in detail but that would need more mental energy than I possess just now. Dickens would have had a wonderful time.

8.00 pm. Here it is – our bedroom, fourposter bed draped with torn and raggy material. Ancient furniture, carpet worn through, surround undusted. Newspaper used to stuff our wet boots dated 1983. When I released the catch on the window to let some air into the room it dropped down like a stone. Bathroom – new bath, loo, washbasin, but dirty hole behind cistern full of rubbish. Cracks in walls, broken catch on door which makes it difficult to lock, dirty tartan carpet on floor. Entrance hall – fierce looking stuffed bear, suit of armour, stuffed birds, filthy carpet on floor. Bar – broken chairs, wobbly tables, bare floorboards, open fire with smoke billowing into the room. Ancient paintings on walls. More stuffed birds, ancient and dirty stone walls. Place absolutely packed with young people, most of whom are smoking, adding to the general fug.

Day 73 – 13th July – Saturday

8.30 am. Came down the baronial stairs into utter darkness and silence. Figures of stuffed bear and knight in armour – suit of armour really – gazed at us out of the gloom. What should we do? I wandered into the kitchen, then – off went the burglar alarm with a piercing shriek. We waited helplessly until suddenly a young girl, scantily dressed, came tearing downstairs saying, 'I'm sorry, I'm sorry, I slept in.' She unlocked the dining room door – the first time we had seen it – but it was in keeping with the rest of the place, full of faded gentility. Stags heads on the walls, tatty polar bear rug on floor. Soggy toast, cold bacon, weak tea.

We were glad to leave. Herbert told the proprietor, who was the smartest part of the set up in full Highland regalia, he had heard the hotel had changed hands and been refurbished. He just smiled.

We left at 10 o'clock in company with another couple we had been meeting at frequent intervals on the West Highland Way, and we all plodded on through the remorseless Scottish rain. Fortunately the terrain was much better than that of yesterday. The authorities were obviously making a real effort to provide walkers with a reasonable path. We stayed on the road until we arrived at Crianlarich about 12.45 pm. Perhaps it was the weather, but this looked a dreary little place. We found a pub where we squeezed our way through crowds of wet walkers and ordered a sandwich. We were soon back into the rain, but not before we had asked the barman whether it ever stopped. Only to be told that 'it hasn't rained here for ages'. (Small comfort to us.) Because of this abysmal weather we stuck to the road after lunch which wasn't much fun but at least it was quick and not muddy. We expected to arrive about 4.30 at Tyndrum, when suddenly Herbert said, 'Here it is.' We had arrived at 3.45 pm. Welcomed by a friendly gentleman, we were shown into a *clean* bedroom and promised a meal at 7.30. What a relief after last night! Mr Cunningham – our host tonight – told us he had heard many stories about Inverarnan House. Some people had found their washbasin coming off the wall and when they turned on the taps the water poured all over the floor. Others found peacocks flying around their bathroom. The birds had come in through a broken skylight and their mess was all over the floor.

Our eagerly awaited homecooked and expensive meal was a bit of a disappointment – just a cold salad – but there was good Scotch Broth and a nice pud. Our wet clothes were dried for us, and our host's wife – who remained unseen – contributed £5 to Christian Aid.

Day 74 – 14th July – Sunday

After breakfast we set off, in good time for once, arriving at Inveroran Hotel at 2.45 pm. We have had a completely dry day which has also been the pleasantest walk so far on the West Highland. Until reaching Bridge of Orchy we were on General Wade's road which was easy walking. We shopped for lunch in Tyndrum before setting off. On route we met a group of volunteers who were spending their holiday repairing the 200-year-old culverts on the old military road in order to preserve the West Highland Way. They were diverting the water which had been flowing down the hillside and which was damaging the paths and breaking down walls. We were told by the leader that the young people actually paid for the privilege. We thanked them all very much for their unselfish labour.

Reaching Bridge of Orchy station we settled down for a peaceful lunch on a convenient seat on the platform. Unfortunately we were joined by a talkative and very boring Yorkshireman who treated us to a monologue about his holiday – he was cycling – which continued until our last mouthful, when we escaped by resuming our walk. It was uphill for a while until the path descended to the hotel. The path was surprisingly dry after so much rain, and there were splendid views all around. We passed above Loch Tulloch, where there was heather-covered moorland and a background of distant mountains. It was very beautiful. But – oh dear – it is a mistake to come back as we discovered two days ago. This hotel, Inveroran Hotel, which we remembered affectionately as a family-run place with open fires and homecooking, has been subjected to 'progress'. No baths, only showers. Toilet access only with a key. Bar meals only – with the all-pervading smell of fried food. In the small, functional bedroom, we found tea, with UDT milk, instructions to walkers on the walls – 'DO NOT put rucksacks on beds'. 'DO NOT wash clothes in hand basins', 'Orders for breakfast at 10.00 pm'. 'Vacate room by 11.00 am.' There is no sense at all of being made welcome. We are much better cared for in the B & Bs. This is the age of mass tourism. There is no individuality. Take what you are given and be thankful. But at least we have a bed and a clean room, and we must keep our eye on the ball and our goal.

9.25 pm. In bed once more after a reasonable meal. There is a sign here, and in most of the places we have stayed along the West Highland Way, which says 'Walkers welcome'. But you do wonder. In addition to the notices on the bedroom walls there are red stickers downstairs instructing walkers how they should behave. We must not bring rucksacks into the hall, bar, etc. Only outer wear can be dried, that is raincoats and boots. Yet walkers comprise the major part of the trade here. Perhaps we are wanted only for our money. We are a 'captive audience', forced to buy expensive food and drink. The brochure of this hotel informed us that the proprietor would give us a friendly welcome, but the only time we saw her was when she took our money before we left. We told her that we didn't feel welcome; she replied that we didn't know how some walkers behaved.

Day 75 – 15th July – Monday After rain during the night it is – at the moment (9.20 am) – mercifully dry.

Today we go over Rannoch Moor to King's House. Again our fond memories may be upset as we have heard poor reports of it from two guests last night. But we will reserve judgement.

2.15 pm. King's House. The rain held off and the 'stroll' over Rannoch (to quote the Shields Gazette's version of our struggle with nature) was rough but otherwise quite easy.

Heavy dark clouds hung around the mountains where it was obviously raining, but we were lucky. Our two friends – the Taylors who have been intermittent companions of the Way – were at Bridge of Orchy last night and fared better than we did. We have seen a lot of walkers today, so the West Highland is becoming ever more popular.

Our fears about King's House have not been realised so far. We have a pleasant room with our own bathroom, which is bliss after last night's miserable shower. There is a hair-dryer and a telephone. What more could we want? But Herbert has a pain in his foot which won't go away. We will try to get some help for this in Fort William.

Day 76 – 16th July – Tuesday

9.00 am. We are still at King's House waiting, as usual, for the rain to stop. We enjoyed our evening here. First we had an excellent meal in a beautiful dining room and then went into the lounge. This is a large room with huge windows on three sides from which we can see across to Rannoch Moor where we had struggled during the day, and over to the impressive mountain Buachaille Etive Mor which rises steeply to a pointed summit. As the sky cleared at last, we watched the pink tinted clouds wafting across the dramatic peak. We chatted to a friendly couple about Scotland, who told us we would see deer beside the hotel if we were to get up early enough. Sadly we had only a view of rooftops from our bedroom.

We wonder what today has in store for us. I massaged Herbert's foot and he is now on pain-killers. What a pity after so many trouble-free miles! We have been in touch with the lady we are staying with in Fort William. She told us there is a lot of mail waiting for us.

3.45 pm. Kinlochleven. Another hard day, up and down hill on a rough path, but we have had some sunshine. It was raining when we started and the mountains had completely disappeared. Five minutes into our walk the rain stopped. The rest of the day alternated between sunshine and showers. We had our lunch at the top of the Devil's Staircase in the company of a group of Germans, and what is more – in hot sunshine. The descent was long and very stony, but there were magnificent views of the mountains all round us. Kinlochleven is the usual shock after the beauties of nature, but we are in a pleasant house and the lady will give us an evening meal. No hot water yet, but we live in hope. Herbert's foot is still painful.

Day 77 – 17th July – Wednesday A bright and sunny morning.

We breakfasted with four Belgians. I had a tickly night as I was covered in midge bites. Our – very fat – hostess talked to us through supper and until we went to bed.

3.45 pm. Another tough day – this gets monotonous doesn't it? At least we had no rain. It was a steep climb out of Kinlochleven, with the compensation of spectacular views back to the mountains. The Way then took us through trees until we reached open country, where there was a high level path along the glen, with mountains on either side. Eventually we reached a forest path which took us to a road junction; there we met the Taylors for the last time. They stayed on the stony footpath. We went on the road which had the double advantage of smoothness and excellent views as we had left the trees. A helicopter was spraying the forest – so we were told by a ranger of the Forestry Commission – with rock phosphate to encourage growth. We shudder to think what this would do to the West Highland Way walkers as the path went through the forest. The ranger also told us that the helicopter cost £600 an hour, and he was doing a time and motion study to see if it was worth it.

The approach to Fort William was from the top of a hill and we could see the whole town and the loch laid out in front of us. We arrived at our B & B in good time and were given a warm welcome. We were told the Minister was coming to see us – he is the CA rep. here. He arrived shortly after we did, heard about Herbert's foot trouble and immediately got in touch with a member of his congregation, a doctor. Within 20 minutes Herbert was in her surgery being examined. 'What can I do for you?' she had asked. 'Keep me going for another fortnight,' was Herbert's reply. So this kind lady has fixed him up with a foot support and some anti-inflammatory cream and said that will get him to John o' Groats.

Our host and hostess are great CA supporters and have been very good to us. They gave us a meal, and refused to take anything for it. They themselves are keen walkers.

Day 78 – 18th July – Thursday

We had a good night, in a comfortable bed. There were letters from Peggie and Lesley.

The next lap of the journey takes us to Inverness. My new 'leather' watch strap has broken. A dull, drizzly morning.

4.45 pm. This morning we bade a fond farewell to Angela and Eric, then went shopping in Fort William. There were queues everywhere – the Post Office, the Bank and Tourist Office – but it is holiday time so we must expect this. We had a sandwich and coffee at a self-service place then set off up the A82. We were not sorry to leave Fort William which is full of tourists. It was drizzle and heavy cloud at first and we could not see the summit of Ben Nevis. The locals said this is the usual state of affairs. By the time we reached the towpath of the Caledonian Canal the sun had come out and we enjoyed the smooth path. As usual there was nothing to eat or drink so we were glad of our early sandwich. After a couple of miles beside the canal we left the towpath for a minor road and continued on this until we reached the A82 again. This minor road was quiet and was so high up above the river that we had spectacular views over the mountainous landscape. Beside a monument put up to commemorate the commandos in the Second World War we rejoined the main road. From this point we were going backwards towards Fort William which was most trying, but the Tourist Board could not get us anywhere else. However, we have had a meal and our hostess let us use her private bath (only showers for guests). We are hoping the young couple we met at dinner will give us a lift up to the top of the hill again. Herbert saw a baby deer on the towpath today. No such luck for me.

Day 79 – 19th July – Friday Spean Bridge. A dull morning. Most days brighten up about midday. We had a noisy night with lorries hurtling past our window. The bed was uncomfortable, but then we get all kinds.

4.15 pm. Invergarry. We left Spean Bridge at 9.30 am and as we had hoped were given a lift up the hill. Our hostess of last night was single-handed – she was barmaid, waitress, cook, washer up, bed maker and mother of two small children. Everything was lavishly generous. There were four pieces of soap instead of the usual one. Heating was put on in our bedroom. There was TV, paper hankies, a slice of lemon in our water jug, about a dozen packets of butter instead of the usual meagre supply. And she gave us £10 for CA. The difference in people's attitudes is amazing. We have walked 14 miles today – mostly on the A82 which is quick but hazardous. Apart from the endless traffic it is a spectacular road, like Lakeland but on a vaster scale. We walked alongside Loch Lochy with great hills on either side, all covered in huge trees and for most of the way the rain held off. Fortunately our hostess had given us some sandwiches because the first restaurant we passed was closed (although a large notice outside offered us coffee, bar lunches, afternoon tea and dinner). Longing for a drink we saw another notice displaying the interesting information that it was open all the year, but underneath was the addition in large letters – 'CLOSED!' Herbert took a photograph of this. At this point we left the road to join the canal once more, and sure enough the cafe beside the lock gates was closed. 'Fridays closed 2.00 pm' it stated on the door. Never mind that it was in fact only ten minutes to two. And another disappointed couple said they had been there since 1.30 pm waiting for it to open. The story of Scotland. We pushed on along the towpath, but unlike that of yesterday, this one was very neglected and overgrown, so much so that it soon became impassable. We managed to escape by scrambling up a steep bank and found a good path higher up. Eventually the A82 again. Still thirsty we came to another encouraging notice, but this time it would have meant a deviation to the loch to find it and we were too tired. A little further on there was the astonishing information, posted in very large letters beside the road, that in 200 m we would come across A SHOP. Sure enough we did. No tea unfortunately, but we bought two cans of cider which certainly helped us to walk the remaining two miles. It began to rain heavily and we had to put on all our waterproofs, but nevertheless we arrived soaked at the Invergarry Hotel where we now are. Our wet rainwear is being dried, we have had a bath and cups of tea and are recovering our equilibrium once more.

10.00 pm. In bed. We ate in the bar which was less impressive than the rest of the hotel, but we shared a table with a young Dutch couple who were interesting company. Returning to the 'posh' part we sat beside a log fire and were entertained by a lively Irish couple. The husband told us a very funny story in a rich brogue. When he was about to leave the lounge he looked hard at us. He said he had passed us on the road and commented to his wife, 'Now there's a pair of professionals.' Then he added, 'I didn't recognise you when you're dressed.' Our smart evening wear always surprises people.

We rang Peggie and Peter.

Day 80 – 20th July – Saturday

We had a good night's sleep, but we were both reluctant to get up. Same old story, dull, heavy cloud, no mountain tops to be seen. But it is not raining at this moment (10.00 am). As we have a shorter day today, only 7 miles, we are not rushing to get going. Breakfast with porridge and 'proper' grapefruit.

As we left the Invergarry Hotel, which is an old-fashioned Victorian place, we saw a vision from another world. Long golden legs, tight mini skirt, high heels, low cut blouse, sculpted golden hair tied with a black bow, red nails and an exquisitely madeup, but quite expressionless face. She was accompanied by a handsome gentleman, either Greek or Cypriot and they drove off in a large black limousine. The girl reminded us of the Bluebell Girls at the Casino in Paris.

After a short stint on the A82 we rejoined the Caledonian Canal and had the good fortune to reach the bridge just as it was opening to let a ship through. Soon after we passed a couple of locks, in one of which there were five boats. There is sophisticated hydraulic machinery to work these, quite unlike the manual locks on the English canals.

We met two American ladies – one quite elderly – on the towpath, and surprisingly they had come all the way from California to walk in Scotland. We told them we had a daughter who had done the reverse, Yorkshire to California.

We met a determined bearded gentleman wearing brief running shorts and a T-shirt with an inscription to say he was supporting a hospice on the Solent. He had just finished John o' Groats to Land's End for this charity. He gave us suggestions for the remainder of our route and told us about the good Scottish soup and cheap accommodation. He had started in trainers which had damaged his feet and forced him to lay up for five days; he was now doing the 60 miles he had missed.

As others see us – a notice we read in a shop.

The Scots kept the Sabbath, and everything else they could lay hands on.

The Welsh prayed on their knees and on everyone else.

The Irish were always fighting but didn't know what about.
The English were a self-made nation, which relieved the Almighty of a dreadful responsibility.

Fort Augustus – 3.00 pm. In sunshine, this little town was a picture. Lovely setting with a canal down the centre, pine-covered hills all round and the southern tip of Loch Ness just appearing. The shops are trippery but quite attractive nevertheless. We had a cup of tea in a little tea shop, with pine furniture and homemade shortbread. Our B & B (quite pricey) is approached by a private road along the Loch. It is a single storey white-painted building just beside Loch Ness. The Old Pier Guest House was once the station house for the railway which met the steamers here. There is a stone patio with tables and chairs and an attractive entrance with a typically Scottish high-pointed tower. Inside it is all pine – floors, furniture, walls. There is a big dining room with large windows overlooking the loch at one end and a fitted kitchen, complete with aga cooker, at the other. There are two large pine tables so that the guests can all eat together. The lounge continues the theme of pine floors and furniture, and we are told that a log fire is lit in the evenings. It is probably a fishing and boating centre rather than one for walkers.

Our hostess could be the headmistress of Cheltenham Ladies College. She is of indeterminate age and wearing ankle socks and a schoolgirl-type skirt and blouse. Her hair is tied back with a ribbon and she has an accent which is certainly not Scottish. She tried hard to be friendly but there seemed to be quite a lot of rules and regulations. When Herbert mentioned the way walkers were treated on the West Highland Way we got the impression her sympathies were not entirely with us. No hot water, we must wait until 5.00 pm for a bath. It is certainly a beautiful position on the edge of Loch Ness.

10.00 pm. Although there was no bath (through an oversight) the lady of the house was very kind to us. We had a tasty homemade meal and good company; a rather dull Scottish couple, but a scintillating Liverpudlian pair. We all sat together at the big table which was very matey. By the time the meal ended, with coffee and Black Magic chocs, we were firm friends. The great coincidence was that the boy from Liverpool, called Peter Davenport, plays football for Sunderland and his training ground is five minutes from our home. He is going to come and see us. Aged 30, he says he is already 'over the top'; he joined the civil service when he was 18, was talent-spotted as an amateur player and became professional, previously playing for Manchester United and Nottingham Forest. His wife, Lesley, is an enchanting little blonde. They are expecting their first baby and are very excited about this. The contrast between this pretty, contented girl and the 'vision', also blonde, of yesterday could not have been greater.

We all met again at breakfast and we left afterwards with great reluctance.

Day 81 – 21st July – Sunday Foyers Bay House.

5.00 pm. The weather has at last relented. There has been no rain and the sun has shone nearly all day. There were little fluffy white clouds, a soft breeze and gentle warmth. We walked back along the loch, then up General Wade's road towards Inverness. This went uphill for 6½ miles but the scenery was sufficient compensation for the slog. As it was clear, we could see for miles – mountains, lochs and pinewoods. We reached the summit of the road about 1.00 pm, just as a tour coach stopped to let its passengers out to look at the view. Herbert asked the driver if he would fill our water bottle. 'No problem,' was the kindly reply.

Across the road an elderly couple were drinking tea in their camping van. We wandered over and engaged them in conversation, and sure enough we were soon offered tea. But we also had to listen to their life history which, although interesting, meant that we had to stand for quite a long time. They were a kindly couple, and after we set off down the hill they overtook us, stopped and took our photographs which they will send to us. (They did and included a donation.)

Ever wearier, we continued until we reached a junction.

Both roads led to Inverness. We took the 'scenic route' which was beautiful, although it meant more hills to climb. Eventually we arrived in Foyers which was approached through alpine scenery, high hills, wide valleys and steep cliffs with cattle grazing so far below us they looked as tiny as toys. We reached the post office and were directed to a forest path leading to the lochside and our place of rest.

This hotel is an odd mixture. We have an elegant bedroom with a spacious private bathroom. There is a bowl of fruit by our bed. The dining room is a conservatory with green imitation marble tables and windows overlooking the garden to Loch Ness. We have enjoyed our meal, but were given chips with our salmon, no fish knives, and salad dressing in plastic packets. The cooking is done at a bar in the dining room and the cook is Italian. The clientele consists mainly of families with lots of noisy children, and the restaurant starts meals at 6.00 pm and closes at 7.30 pm.

Day 82 – 22nd July – Monday Day dawned dry but dull, the sunshine of yesterday has fled.

We had the same table for breakfast and a Belgian family started talking to us for so long that finally mine host politely asked us to leave as he had to clean the restaurant before lunch.

Our walk today continued along the scenic route to Inverness but was not so dramatic as yesterday. It was a long slog between tall trees with occasional glimpses of Loch Ness, where there were picnic places. There were notices at these saying 'Please take your litter home', which people certainly did as there was none lying about. As for us, there was no picnic. As usual we had seen no shops, cafes or pubs – which is probably the reason for the cleanliness everywhere. About one o'clock we stopped and ate the fruit we had found in our hotel bedroom and some shortbread left over from yesterday. There were few walkers, but one couple – a mother and son – appeared and, as always, we stopped and spoke to them. What an extraordinary sight! They were Austrians who lived in the Tirol. 'Why come here,' we asked, 'when you have such beautiful scenery?' She said it was good to see how other people lived, and to learn about other traditions. This lady carried a large handbag, had a very large rucksack on her back and wore a Loch Ness monster bracelet on her arm. But what really amazed us were her open-toed sandals (through which we observed bright blue toe nails), and they were walking to Mallaig from Inverness – 120 miles.

We arrived in Dores soon after 3 o'clock, found a pub which is superior by Scottish standards, had a toasted sandwich and listened to some Scottish music for a change. As there was no-one in at our B & B we sat on the doorstep until the lady turned up. This is another good place with PFs. There is only a shower, but I was allowed to use the family's private bath (which was luxurious). This took all the hot water so Herbert had a cold shower.

Early today we missed the path and landed up on a private road through a hydro-electric works. 'No admittance for unauthorised persons', a notice stated curtly. So one unauthorised person asked at the gatehouse if we could walk through. 'Ask Mike Whitefield, the station superintendent.' We couldn't find this character but a man with his peaked cap the wrong way was anxious to oblige. We told him our usual tale – old people, very tired, too far to go back, walking from Land's End to John o' Groats, etc, etc. 'Good grief!' was the astounded reply. We got through.

Most of the day we have been accompanied by the sound of screaming jets.

6.30 pm. Back in the pub for our evening meal. Good home cooking (no chips for once).

* * *

The Roadwalking Experience

During the early stages of planning, our guide and encourager, Mac, wrote us a letter in which he said that his worst experience was the one day when he walked down the A74 into Carlisle (remember, he was doing it the other way round). This made us all the more determined to keep off roads, and Herbert worked late into many a night poring over the maps, especially of Scotland, searching for those minute lines which might provide alternatives. And the original plan, already detailed, did provide alternatives for most of the distance. Only the A74 and the A9 remained undecided when we set off. It is, of course, one thing to plan a walk in a domestic setting, sitting dry and warm and comfortable in your favourite armchair over a roaring fire, and quite a different matter when it comes to putting it into practice, especially when the weather lets you down continually, for weeks on end. That is why the diary so often tells a different story from those best-laid plans, and why we spent a great deal more time walking along roads than we ever intended. We have already admitted that there were times when we were making such heavy weather of some of the footpaths that we transferred to the roads just to get a move on. But the principal reason was without doubt the weather. It is possible to plough through bog and slush and 'clarts' (a good Northumbrian word) for a day or two, or even a week or two – walkers regularly endure such conditions for the whole length of the Pennine Way – but when you are walking a thousand miles or more you think differently. You think discretion, which is the better part of valour. You think of your footwear, for instance. That poor sucker in the Guardian who walked from Cape Wrath and lost the sole off a boot after a few days – the reason for that was that he had walked through those few days in pouring rain and across the most sodden terrain imaginable. Road walking became a necessity just to conserve some of our resources. We later heard from a couple of the Pennine Way walkers we met (it's always the PW isn't it? Why does anyone walk it?) that Cross Fell was just about the end of all hope; they felt like sitting down and giving up altogether.

Assuming therefore, that some of you grandparents will be taking to the road, we thought we should offer you the benefit of our experience. Is it dangerous? is Question Number One. Many were the times when we looked upon the flattened remains of some poor unobservant rabbit or a hedgehog which shouldn't have attempted it in the first place, and thought to ourselves, 'There but for the grace of God . . .' But it doesn't happen that way. We were reminded of a dear friend in Naples, Giuseppi Gallozzi, called Joe for short, who would see you were hesitating on the edge of the pavement as you wondered how on earth you would ever get across to the other side of that battlefield of motor cars; he would take you firmly by the arm, march you across in front of those screaming motorists, protesting with the full strength of their horns, and to the accompaniment of screeching tyres and brakes; and he would say, with complete confidence, 'Don't worry, they won't kill you.' They didn't kill us; in fact there were times when the concern for our safety was quite touching. The drivers where possible would slow down and move out, and wave in gratitude if you had stopped on the verge.

Of course there are roads and roads, and we walked most of them. There was that Devon road where we could sit down in the middle to eat an apple. There was the A39 into Bideford which had recently been rebuilt in the most civilised fashion, with little private lanes for cyclists at the side, which we could use, free from the usual perils. There were straight roads and winding roads, and uphill roads and level roads, country roads and town roads; each one had its own individual problems which demanded individual diagnosis and individual solutions. For instance, do you walk on the left side of the road or the right side? The right, you say, because you are facing the oncoming traffic. But not always, dear reader. There were times when we would be walking along the right, with not a car in sight and not a care in the world, when, whoosh! one of those mad joyriders comes tearing past you on the wrong side of the road having just overtaken some innocent, law-abiding driver who was getting in his way. They were probably the greatest threat to our safety because there was no way of anticipating them. Again, on the A74, right was wrong and left was right, if you get the meaning. Walking into the traffic you were continually buffetted by the air stream which accompanies the lines of heavy vehicles pounding along at full speed. Indeed there was a real danger of being sucked into the road, and we didn't like it at all. It was a bit like the Geordie who, having been told that he would have to drive on the right on the Continent, tried it out in this country and pronounced it 'bloody dangerous'. So we walked with the traffic on the A74 and found that the great rush of wind generated by HGVs actually helped us along.

In a strange way, we became quite attached to the A74. There were drivers who obviously did it daily and it wasn't long before these two whitehaired hikers with purple rucksacks were being recognised as part of the regular scene; lights were flashed at us and horns hooted and cheers echoed from passing vehicles. Even the police waved to us. We felt we had become part of the fellowship.

The sequel to the A74 was, of course, walking through Glasgow which was a most miserable experience and was without doubt the low point of the journey. Perhaps it was the contrast with the open and empty spaces which we had walked for over two months, or the contrast between the natural world and the man-created world. Could we have avoided Glasgow? If you are going to walk the West Highland the answer is certainly no, but next time . . .

After that the roads were child's play. As we progressed up Scotland we realised the benefit of so many foreign visitors – they were much better at judging the distances between us and them, thanks to their left-hand drive. We discovered the benefits of the multitude of caravans, especially those parked in lay-bys for the purposes of tea-brewing. Look thirsty as you pass and invariably you were invited to partake. The A9 provided no such dramatic diversion as it did for Joss Ackland who discovered a lorry off the road and was delayed for a day as a result. For us it was that shining path leading to the Celestial City, and we hurried along it with ever more hope and eagerness until – well, read on and the diary will tell you.

* * *

Day 83 – 23rd July – Tuesday Very wet first thing.

Today we have only 8 miles to Inverness, where we meet the CA representative outside Marks and Spencer. My word – we are getting fit. We covered the 8 miles from Dores to Inverness in $2\frac{1}{2}$ hours. The rain held off and the road was mostly downhill; we had an easy passage, but are promised some difficult hills along the coast.

Herbert guided us expertly to the B & B, and our impressions of Inverness were very favourable. We walked alongside the river, with a colourful park on the other side. The flowerbeds full of vivid colours were the first we had seen since Moffat. We crossed the river on a footbridge and found a good place to eat our sandwiches. After some necessary shopping in a crowded pedestrian precinct, entirely free of litter, we met the Perth CA representative, John Wylie, who had travelled over a hundred miles to see us. He took us to the local Methodist minister's house where we received the kindest hospitality from Rev. Derek Sutcliffe and his wife. This is a very good day. We had left most of our belongings at our B & B, which is another excellent place – our own bathroom, a pretty bedroom and, even better, an evening meal. Derek Sutcliffe brought us back by car, and on the way showed us his church. This is a grand, modern building with beautiful stained-glass windows, including one of John Wesley on his horse. The Inverness CA representative, Frank Spaven, came to see us at the Manse and he and John Wylie are trying to arrange accommodation for us further north, so we are getting a lot of help. There was a long letter from Helen, with a parcel of clean clothes waiting for us in our B & B here, also one from Peggie. All well at home.

8.00 pm. We are the only ones in for dinner, although our host kept turning people away as he had no more beds. It is now holiday time and accommodation is getting more difficult. Another appetising meal. How will I ever start cooking again?

* * *

The Beginning of the End

Day 84 – 24th July – Wednesday Inverness. Brilliant sunny morning, but for how long we wonder . . . not long, about one hour.

Mr Hunter, who served our dinner last night, told us he took part in a team effort a few years ago which ran from Land's End to John o' Groats in ten days. Two teams ran 100 miles a day.

Herbert rang Frank Spaven, the local CA rep, who has fixed up a bed for us in a private house at Culbokie. This means we have been able to get off the A9 onto a minor road. Frank also came and guided us through the streets of Inverness as far as the Kessock Bridge on the Beauly Firth. Just before the bridge we saw our first sign to John o' Groats – 126 miles – which was a great excitement. (In fact the signpost is wrong, it should be 136.) We said goodbye to our kind guide and walked across this marvellous bridge high up

Inverness

above the wide firth, with vistas across to Inverness behind us and the Black Isle ahead. At the Tourist Information on the other side of the bridge we obtained free literature about the way ahead. A man with a Scottish tie and an English accent asked us how far we were going and whether he could help us. He had a van and was ferrying tourists about. We declined his offer reluctantly.

We are now in a pub in Mullochy, having walked 7 miles along a rather dull country road. The weather has deteriorated and there is a thundery feel about it. Frank is trying to persuade the local telly to come and find us, but they are probably too preoccupied with the merger of the Gordon Highlanders and another Scottish regiment – just announced by the Government – which is of far greater significance to the Scots than the exploits of elderly English walkers.

1.45 pm. After our lunch we continued along the same rather uninteresting road until we decided to sit by the roadside and have a drink of water. All of a sudden a young man got out of his car and asked us the usual question, 'Where are you going?' 'Culbokie.' 'Like a lift?' We once again had to explain why we could not accept. 'Well,' he said cheerfully, 'come and see old Jock, he'll give you a cup of tea.' Before we knew what was happening he had led us into a little shack made of corrugated iron which we had just walked past (and had wondered who could possibly live there). It was dirty, smelly and shabby (but had an aerial photograph of the establishment on the wall). Old Jock, aged 86, who had lived there all his life and brought up a family of five, is now living alone in this shack. He and Duncan, the young man who had offered the hospitality, and Chris, a scruffy cyclist we had previously seen on the road, all smoked continuously so that we could hardly see across the room. But we were given a mug of steaming tea and some biscuits, which old Jock threw down in front of us onto a table. We had a very happy time. Duncan's philosophy – Don't take life too seriously. When things get bad, just laugh about them. They can only get better.

* * *

Culbokie. Our private accommodation is a revelation. After leaving our 'tea shop' we walked for half an hour, missed the vital turning and had an extra mile to do, but arrived eventually at the house of the minister at Culbokie who, we had been promised, would arrange a bed for us. This was the Rev. J. McLeod. He was formerly in India working for Christian Aid, and was particularly concerned with agriculture. He came back to England, searching for water-drilling machinery (originally rock was blasted away with gelignite). He stayed with a friend in Halifax and the subject cropped up. His friend said they had just installed a drill in their works, manufactured in Halifax. John McLeod went to this firm which made drills principally for quarrying, and ended up by arranging to buy two. The firm, discovering it was for Christian Aid, gave them a third free. John wanted to publish the story in CA News, but the director told him not to because 'the shareholders wouldn't like it'. The machines were ideal for what was needed and eventually the firm's total output went to charities working in third world areas. We told John there were constant reservations from the people we talked to whether the money they gave ever got through to those who needed it – Eritrea for example. He was angry about this and said that generally people did not understand the positive results. He cited the example of blasting rock for water in India – the rock being cleared away by women – until finally the water gushed out. An Indian beside him put his arm round his shoulder and started weeping. He knew that his life and the lives of his family were no longer dependent on when or whether the rains came; that he could keep a few goats and sheep, grow orange trees and crops, and their future livelihood was assured. That is what Christian Aid means. The money given doubles in value.

After this long talk with Mr McLeod, he drove us to our place of rest – the home of two members of his congregation where we were received with great kindness. The meal was complemented by homemade wine, and afterwards our host, Peter, massaged our feet, telling us at the same time about the mission of his wife and himself to be counsellors to the people of Culbokie. We felt this would prove to be a hard task as our host and hostess were 'foreigners' – both being Yorkshire people!

Day 85 – 25th July – Thursday A fine, sunny morning.

Our kind hostess gave us breakfast while our host continued to talk non-stop, even standing over us while we were packing. After mutual photograph taking he drove us back to our point of entry – five miles – and since then we have walked across the bridge over the Cromarty Firth, then alongside the water on the A9. At 11.30 am we found the only place to eat so had our sandwiches early today.

4.25 pm. Alness. We are now in a poor little fish and chip shop where we are drinking tea. The only tea shop was – of course – closed. It has been a perfect afternoon with clear blue skies. After our long rest at lunchtime (we had two hours just lying in the sunshine beside the firth) we left the A9 and followed a minor road to this dreary town where we are staying the night with the local minister. An old man stopped and offered us a lift. Our usual reply resulted in a long conversation and the story of his life. He is a retired Yorkshireman (another one) living near his daughter and son-in-law, who is the minister of the 'Wee Free Kirk'. This gentleman is a keen cricketer, so Herbert was happy. After this interlude we continued along a pleasant leafy road and then wended our way uphill to the town where, after tea, we kept our rendezvous at the station with the minister at 6.00 pm.

Day 86 – 26th July – Friday Dull morning – disappointing after yesterday.

Bill Niven, our host, and his wife Agnes, looked after us well. After a bath and a meal we listened to records of Scottish music, which was very pleasant. They live in a modern house on an estate. It is high up and overlooks the Cromarty Firth. They have two daughters, one in London, the other a missionary in Pakistan. Mrs Niven is very nationalistic and, we suspect, not terribly fond of the English, which is not altogether surprising in view of our turbulent history.

Bill took us to the start of our walk today which was 12 miles along a minor road. There were quite a number of houses dotted about which were all new and almost identical. Apparently you can get a kit, employ a builder to lay the foundations, then build it yourself.

White Settlers. This is the name given by the Scots to people from England, usually the southern part, who have sold their houses at a huge profit, migrated to Scotland and bought (or built) a house here. According to our host last night they stay on average a couple of winters, then find the climate too harsh and move back again. This view was borne out today. We met a lady walking her dog on the lonely road we were on. She stopped to speak to us and was obviously English. She said she lived 'down the road' and sure enough when we reached it there was a notice, 'For sale, house and 15 acres'.

5.00 pm. Tain. We continued along the same straight road after our lunch break. It became hot and sticky, so it was a relief to arrive at our B & B. The lady here is suffering from bronchitis and seemed very miserable. She can't give us a meal so we must go to the village and take pot luck. Unlike most Scottish houses, this one is a large two-storeyed, stonebuilt building, probably Victorian. We have a large bedroom with a double bed and a single, a settee and chair, washbasin – there's plenty of room for the daily unloading of our possessions. We can relax here and do not have to make polite conversation as we had to the last two nights. There is an open view from the window across fields to the Cromarty Firth and we can see for miles along the coast where we will be heading for the next few days. The more numerous single-storeyed houses we see everywhere are all alike, and we wondered whether the builder had run out of bricks and just put the roof on.

We were in luck this evening as we hit upon a superior hotel where we had good Scottish salmon. The barman and waitress wished us well on hearing of our venture. We rang Jane, being desperate for our second pair of boots, but again there was no reply. Where was our coordinator? Rang Helen, who is busy packing up for their Scottish holiday tomorrow, and learned that Jane and family got back from California on Wednesday, went to the Isle of Man on Thursday, returning Monday and are then going to Germany and France. We'll have to make do.

Day 87 – 27th July – Saturday Fine, dry morning. High cloud, but no sun.

We had a good night in a firm bed, although there was noisy traffic outside. Marmalade with whisky for breakfast. We are going back to Tain to do some shopping, then back along the A9 to the B & B to pick up our rucksacks. When we told our hostess we were going to the village, she said indignantly, 'It's not a village, it's a royal burgh.'

Our hostess, Mrs Roberts, whose bronchitis was better, was very talkative and our departure was delayed. She told us, among other things, that one of her customers was an old lady of 78 who was doing Land's End to John o' Groats on a tricycle, in company with her dog, to raise money for an old people's home.

Our great excitement today has been walking across the new bridge over the Dornoch Firth. It is not yet open but we set off in the hope that we wouldn't be turned back as the bridge would save us 22 miles. The engineer in charge was driving over the bridge in his car and stopped as we approached. 'Can I help you?' he asked politely. We, rather nervously, made our request, and he replied simply, 'No problem.' He also said we should be careful, as there were men working on the bridge and we might get covered with paint. We came across these men who were not working but sitting down and chatting to one another. This is the longest bridge of its type in Britain. We talked to a man with a paintbrush laboriously painting the railings; we commiserated with him and he said each railing along this vast bridge had to have four coats of paint. If at any time in the next twenty years his wife should suggest he did some painting in the house he would shoot her.

Leaving the bridge we continued along the new road until we reached the roundabout connecting the bridge with the A9. After being entirely alone we were once again amongst traffic.

After many hours on this road, with a brief stop for a picnic, we reached the pub at Poles where we are staying tonight. There is a pleasant sitting room for residents and we had a friendly chat with a young Scottish family. On hearing our destination for tomorrow they said, 'Oh, that's not far.' 'It is when you're walking,' we answered.

Day 88 – 28th July – Sunday A fine, sunny morning which is miraculous as there was heavy rain in the night.

We left Poles at 9.00 am – an early start for our long day. So far the A9 has been fairly quiet and quite picturesque. There are wide views all round – to the right the Firth, to the left high, pine-covered hills. We crossed 'The Mound' after an hour and a half. This is a new causeway which dams the river across most of its width. There is a huge inlet from the sea, but it was low tide when we crossed and all we saw

North Sea

were large areas of mud flats. There was a notice on the roadside warning drivers to beware of wildlife, but as has been our experience throughout our walk, we saw nothing except rabbits, both running around and dead on the road. The nearest we have got to stags or deer has been the large stag's head on the wall of the pub in Golspie where we are at this moment having our lunch.

My back trouble is much improved today. It is marvellous how these things come and go. We have shed some of our possessions, and will post a few more home tomorrow, which will make the last stretch easier.

Just as we were leaving the new bridge yesterday three workmen in a car stopped and offered us a lift – that makes four in all since we started.

4.30 pm. Brora. We are in another upmarket B & B, with PFs. We have been on the A9 all day, but as it is Sunday it hasn't been at all bad. Sometimes there has been no traffic at all on the road. Once past The Mound we had the sea on our right – glistening and glinting in the sunlight. We made a brief stop at Dunrobin Castle to look at the famous gardens, but had no strength left for touring the rooms.

Just as we reached Brora, which is a rather ordinary seaside town, a man in a touring van drove up, got out and approached us. 'Are you the two walkers to John o' Groats?' he asked. We both thought the telly had caught us up. No. It was a member of the Inverness Methodist Church. The minister had mentioned us from the pulpit during the morning service – the message of the sermon was about never being too old . . . – and quite a lot of money was being raised by the congregation for CA. We needed that encouragement.

Day 89 – 29th July – Monday

There is a curious class distinction in many Scottish hotels between the bar and the rest of the building. Both in the Glengarry Hotel in Invergarry and in the Links at Brora last night we have had a culture shock on walking through a door marked Bar Lounge. It was, in both places, like going from a luxurious house into a slum. Never mind, we had a cheap meal which wasn't at all bad. The restaurant was charging £17.50.

9.45 am. I am sitting on a bench in the sunshine guarding both rucksacks while Herbert is trekking back to the post office to send some surplus clothing home. I now have only one pair of shorts and one thin cardigan. But reducing weight at this stage seems a good idea. We had a good bed and breakfast at our smart B & B, and now we are about to set off again along the east coast of Scotland. As I look I see the familiar east coast mist rolling in. But there's not going to be any rain which is the main thing. Our ministerial accommodation doesn't seem to be working too well, but a lady in the tea shop told us yesterday that we just needed to knock on the door of any cottage and either they would take us in, or would find someone else who could. That should be fun.

5.20 pm. The Bridge Hotel in Helmsdale, Caithness. This has been a magical day. Although we have continued along the A9 it was not very busy, and has led us through wonderful scenery. After leaving Brora we walked along the coastal path with the golf course on our left. Grass was growing almost to the water's edge, and we were amused to see a herd of cattle actually on the beach drinking the salt water puddles. After crossing the railway line (along which we will soon be returning home) we rejoined the road which wound its way up and down, sometimes high above the sea, at other times right beside it. There has been a cloudless blue sky, a little hazy but no mist, and a soft breeze to keep us cool. It was perfect. We found a little hidden dell in which to eat our cheese and biscuits (donated by our landlady from last night) and we both went sound asleep.

As we journeyed along the last five miles of the day we reached Port Gower which was the only habitation we passed all day other than a few scattered crofts. We were gasping for a drink and thought that there would be a shop. But, no luck. A white haired gentleman was standing talking to two young people (who we discovered later were his granddaughter and son) and he said as we passed, 'It's a guid dee for a walk,' and, with the thought uppermost in my mind, I said, 'Oh yes, but is there anywhere where we could get a cup of tea?' 'Why, come along in and I'll make you some,' he said spontaneously. He invited us into his pretty little garden, pointed out a wooden seat, and hurried indoors to make the tea. He soon re-appeared with a tray of tea, homemade cake and biscuits.

It would take a long time to recount all that he told us this afternoon. Owing to an injury sustained many years ago he had great trouble with his back, so he did not sit down, but just leaned on the garden table (which, like the wooden bench we were sitting on, he had made himself), and talked and talked in a soft Highland brogue. He had lived most of his life in Bonar Bridge, which was his family home for four generations. His name was Hector Calder, although he used the Gallic form. His first wife had been an invalid most of their married life and had died just after their silver wedding. After three years he had remarried. His second wife has a job at an old people's home, and he kept looking at his watch as if he were hoping she would come home before we left. He told us some heartrending stories about the poverty and depopulation of the Highlands, how there had been a Conservative Government for twelve years which had done nothing for Scotland. He told us of the injustice of making an old lady, who lived alone in a house with no running water or electricity, pay the same poll tax as he, who had modern conveniences. The fact that she possessed some cattle made her ineligible for relief. Hector also talked about the difficulty his granddaughter had in getting to school. There were no bus shelters and roads were often snowed up. He had written to his MP who was sympathetic, but helpless. 'There are so many in the same position', was his reply. This gentle Highlander was bitter about the aristocracy and wealthy people from the south who fenced off vast areas of land (where apparently there are untapped goldmines) because they wanted it for hunting and shooting. It was all very sad, and we wanted to do something to help – but what can be done? Agriculture and fishing used to be the mainstay of the region and now farmers were being paid to stop producing.

After he had come to the end of all this he wanted to show

us round his garden which, although small, seemed to grow every conceivable fruit and vegetable. While we were passing his strawberry bed he found two birds caught in the netting and he very gently released them. He had been a stonemason and showed us some of his work, including some bizarre little figures. He had also been a gamekeeper on a big estate for many years, and had worked as a pest controller for the council. A fascinating man. We were introduced to his neighbour, a young woman who, he said, had just been divorced, and both of them gave us a donation for our cause. Before we left he gave us his phone number and asked us to ring him up when we got home. We would be very welcome to come and see him at any time, he told us when we parted.

The road down into Helmsdale reminded us of the Amalfi coast with its twists and turns. Ahead lay the village, perched high up on the cliffs; the sea was a deep blue and the sands golden. It is difficult to believe we are so far north.

This so-called hotel, although large, is really a glorified pub with the inevitable smell of fried food. We decided to try somewhere else to eat but the restaurant opposite the hotel which advertised outside 'salmon hot or cold, cooked as you wish', had no salmon. We dined in the hotel after all and it turned out to be better than expected.

Day 90 – 30th July – Tuesday A fine but overcast morning.

Herbert's boots are worn right down but as Jane has vanished nothing can be done about them. We have booked in at the hotel in John o' Groats (Peter de Savary's). Herbert told the proprietor we were walking. 'Good God,' was the reply.

5.40 pm. Dunbeath (c/o Mrs Sutherland, Lou to her friends). The first hour today was sunny and the road spectacular as it snaked its way around the hills, upwards and downwards, with hairpin bends, and always in sight of the sea. Unfortunately the Scottish 'haar' came down and we were soon enveloped in thick mist, which continued for the rest of the day. We lost our views of the countryside and it was just a question of keeping going. About ten o'clock we descended steeply to Berrivale, via Berrivale Brae. There was a post office at the bottom and one or two houses, also a bus shelter with a seat, which was an improvement on the telephone box on the West Highland Way. We sat down and ate our picnic which we had prudently bought before we left Helmsdale. Then it was a steep climb upwards on another series of hairpins (where Joss Ackland came across the crashed vehicle in the film 'The First and the Last'). We had been warned about this climb but found it comparatively easy now that we are in good training. We trudged on and on and on in the fog until we came across something that called itself a snack bar. There was nowhere to sit down so we bought some orange juice and walked on, reaching Dunbeath after about seven hours. Here there was a place where we could get tea, and have a seat. We were told that Joss Ackland and the film crew used to go in while they were filming. Herbert set off in search of a B & B which a lady we met in the village told us about. Here we are in heaven! Mrs Sutherland has taken us in, we have had a hot bath and are now sitting beside a roaring peat fire. She has agreed to give us our breakfast tonight (like Buxton) and there is a table covered with a dainty cloth and lots of goodies. We are glad we didn't go to the hotel here.

Only 38 miles left to do. This morning we met our friend Hector again in Helmsdale.

9.45 pm. We have had an amazing evening. Lou, our hostess produced bacon, egg, sausage, baked beans, potatoes (home-grown), toast, white and brown bread, home-made raspberry jam, drop scones, fairy cakes, shortbread, rock cakes and a very large pot of tea with extra teabags. We were both very hungry and did justice to the banquet. After this was cleared away we chatted with Lou and Jim, her husband, also with another couple who have stayed here many times and were very friendly with the two Highlanders. Later a Swiss couple turned up. They were revisiting Lou and Jim with whom they had spent a previous holiday. At about 9 o'clock tables were put out, more tea arrived with more cakes and sandwiches. We could not manage much this time. When we said we must go to bed Lou came with us, switched on an electric blanket (there's a duvet and three blankets on the bed) and said she would bring us a cup of tea bed in the morning. (Jim described himself as the dish-washer on two legs, and the best toast maker in Scotland.)

Day 91 – 31st July – Wednesday The ante-penultimate.

We have just been awakened with tea and biscuits. This is a four star establishment. There is still thick fog outside, but the forecasters have promised us sunshine this afternoon. Let us hope they are right.

We have had breakfast beside the peat fire, and Lou has given us oranges and Mars bars. This is hospitality on a mammoth scale. The charge – £5 per person. As we were leaving I said to Lou, 'If we ever write a book you'll be in it.' She said, 'We've been in two already.'

12.00 noon. Lybster. As promised by the weatherman the fog has cleared and at the moment the sun is struggling to get through the clouds. We have now walked seven miles from Dunbeath and are so fit we have hardly noticed. As we walked we passed many abandoned crofts with tall weeds growing almost up to the low roofs. In a few years they will surely disappear altogether. But there are hopeful signs as well, as there are a number of new buildings, all of the same single storey design, often with a car standing outside. Perhaps this most northern corner of the British Isles is not so poverty stricken as the abandoned crofts suggest. In some places a new one has been built in front of the old; in others the family seem to live in a large modern caravan which is parked beside the ancient croft with the broken window and holed roof. The explanation – crofters receive grants for rebuilding but not repairing, so the old ones are allowed to decay.

After lunch we found that the skies had cleared. We had an invigorating high level walk with enormous views of sky, sea and moors. Rang Carr House from a telephone box (unexpected in this remote area). They go to Papenburg on

Sunday so we won't be seeing them at John o' Groats. As the afternoon wore on we started looking for a bed, but after the morning's profusion there was nothing. We knocked on the door of a couple of cottages – no-one in. Herbert was getting worried. Then about 4 o'clock we saw what we thought was a hopeful sign on a house. As we got nearer we realised it was a 'For sale' notice. A little further we were relieved to see the welcome blue B & B and even better, EM. The sign pointed to a left turn up a hill. There were a couple of houses on the way up but neither was the one we were seeking. We turned a corner and there it was – an idyllic place overlooking a beautiful loch. The house is a modern bungalow and outside are hundreds of alpine plants for sale. A few cars were parked outside when we arrived and we wondered if the B & B was full up. We rang the bell and a youngish Englishman came to the door. 'Have you a double room?' asked Herbert. He smiled, 'For you, yes.' Within seconds his wife appeared, showed us into a pretty room and soon afterwards we were sitting in deckchairs on a patio drinking tea. We sat for about an hour in the sunshine enjoying the scenery, then had a bath in yet another luxurious bathroom. Jane, our hostess, gave us a wonderful meal, let down only by the Nescafe, after which we sat in an attractive sitting room reading, then chatting to Andrew, their 18-year-old son. His hobby is karate, which he was pleased to demonstrate for us. He works at Dounreay Nuclear Power Station and said it was a relief to come back to this peaceful place after working there. Terry and Jane moved up from Northampton where they had a nursery for alpines. They love Caithness. The people are so much nicer than the English, they told us. Terry was very anxious to impress on us that they were integrated and accepted by the locals. But I wonder. It probably takes many generations to become part of this close-knit Highland society. Terry told us the people here are very bad drivers, and we heard his horrific story. This house has a self-contained annex where Terry's mother came to live after selling her house in Kent. He was driving her one day – she was in the back without a seatbelt on – when a mini appeared on the wrong side of the road. He swerved to avoid it and went into a deep ditch on the other side. His mother was thrown out and killed.

Day 92 – 1st August – Thursday The penultimate.

The fog had come down again during the night and we could see nothing of the loch when we left Terry and Jane this morning. We walked into Wick without being able to see anything except a few yards of the road ahead. To our great joy we bumped into Lou and Jim in Wick who greeted us like long-lost friends. They were just coming out of a supermarket having done their week's shopping. We went to the Tourist Information place in Wick but they could give us little help. A Mrs Harrold had a guest house, they believed, but as she wasn't on their list they could not contact her. We went rather disconsolately on our way, thinking that perhaps we would have to do the whole distance to John o' Groats today. We plodded on mile after mile along the straight road. Although the fog lifted the sky was still overcast and gloomy and the countryside did not glisten as it did yesterday. It is becoming very flat now, and we could see the sand dunes beside the sea as there are no cliffs here. Eventually we arrived at the B & B which the tourist people had told us about, and were in luck as there was a free room. This is another modern bungalow and the room is clean and nicely furnished. We missed the very warm welcome that Terry and Jane had given us but Mrs Harrold was willing to give us bacon and eggs at 6 o'clock when we told her we were too tired to walk the two miles to the hotel which she had suggested. There was no tea on offer when we arrived – the first time for 92 days – but we have taken a big slice out of tomorrow's walk. It is now only 10 miles to our final destination.

10.00 pm. Mrs Harrold has been as kind as most of our hosts have been. We had a satisfying high tea, and then went into the sitting room where we met a Swiss family. 'I hope I can do as well when I'm your age,' said Father. Mrs Harrold and her husband built this house themselves 27 years ago and have done B & B for 21 years. She produced tea and cakes for everyone at 9 o'clock (which we couldn't eat). I am sure foreigners must be impressed by British B & Bs.

Day 93 – 2nd August – Friday The ultimate.

7.30 am fog again. 8.50 am fog clearing.

It was a sunny morning until about eleven. We could see for miles in all directions as the road climbed steadily uphill. We stopped at a little shop for a picnic which we ate very early as we could see the clouds coming in from the west. There were a number of abandoned and derelict crofts beside the road; as we went further north even these disappeared and there was nothing to be seen but wild moorland. The A9 got narrower, road markings disappeared as though even the road knew it was nearing the end. As we reached the top of the last incline we saw the Orkney Islands spread out in front of us. We paused a while, hardly able to believe we had walked the length of the British Isles. After this emotional moment it was all downhill to our final destination. Arrived at John o' Groats 1.45 pm. The town was not a disappointment as we had been told it was dull. But the hotel is a real anti-climax. It is a very rundown place. It seems Peter de Savary, who owns the wonderful State House at Land's End, has decided not to spend anything on it as he has plans to pull it down and rebuild it. But all that matters is – we've made it. We had our picture taken, the children have sent us a bottle of champagne, Tom Bennett has sent us a hand-drawn card, . . . and we don't have to walk tomorrow.

Epilogue

'Did you enjoy it?' – the question everyone asks. Reading through the diary imaginatively it is not difficult to identify occasions when the answer is very obviously 'No'. It is always worth reminding yourself of Gladys's philosophy in the Himalayas – 'True enjoyment is the experience of contrasts' – and there are few greater pleasures in life than taking off your boots after a long, hard day, and drinking tea, and lying in a steaming bath, and eating a meal you haven't cooked (and drinking more tea), and flopping into bed to sleep for eight, nine, ten hours. But it isn't the all-important question that most people seem to think it is. You don't set out on a walk from Land's End to John o' Groats just to enjoy yourself. There are many simpler, easier and cheaper ways of doing that. The notion of challenge has already been mentioned, and it would be sheer humbug to pretend that you don't end up with a certain sense of achievement. That, like enjoyment, is an overused word today and doubtless there are easier ways of realising it as well. Maybe you get nearer the truth if you read the starry eyed romanticism of Tennyson's 'Ulysses' in which the wanderer, now an old man, just cannot sit around at home in idleness and uselessness. So off he goes once again, 'to follow knowledge like a sinking star beyond the utmost bound of human thought'.

That's the stuff to wallow in if you are a sentimentalist. Even in these days of rationalism and materialism and all the other 'isms', it is still possible to hear the call of the great unknowns and untrieds of life, which was the fire smouldering in the breast of Joss Ackland as he set out from the First to the Last. You don't have to walk to hear that call; it may come through art or music or learning of any sort; some of us might hear it on the cricket field. But however and wherever it comes it has to be heeded. You set out on some great venture not because you are seeking enjoyment or achievement, but because you are 'grasped', taken over by the cause to which you are committed.

Duncansby Head

Of course there are joys and pleasures in the unparalleled variety of beauty this land of ours possesses, much of which we were seeing for the first time. But there were satisfactions deeper even than that experience – for instance, the fact that we did it together. The walk is a parable of that life we have shared for over forty years, with its ups and downs, its sunshine and rain. We are grateful to the God who made us that He made us for mutual support, which enables us to do things together which we could never do on our own. We are grateful for health and strength as well; we realise how fortunate we are that our legs can keep moving and all the necessary components work as they were intended.

One feature which stands out more than the scenery – and this will have been abundantly evident in the pages of the diary – is the kindness of the people we met. An unfortunate fact of life today is that your conception of your fellow men and women is coloured to a great extent by the media. Once, you discovered human nature by meeting it; now you are content to read about it or watch it perform on the telly. This is a form of brainwashing which eventually convinces you that society is peopled by perverts and thieves and muggers, and all the most unpleasant specimens of humanity imaginable. The walk tells a different story; everywhere you go you are met by kindness and consideration and generosity and love. You walk through a wonderful world.

It was difficult to stop. The following day we made the great mistake of taking a trip to the Orkneys. Under cloudless skies and surrounded by brilliant sea we were squashed like the proverbial sardines into hot smelly buses full of noisy humanity and children sucking ice lollies. It was too soon for that. The day after, when we were to catch the train home, we awoke at 5.30 in the morning when again the sun was shining and the sea sparkling. So we upped and offed on our own two feet to Duncansby Head, the extreme northeast corner of mainland Britain, and there in the early morning solitude we realised again that sense of magic which disappears so quickly once you get back into the ruts of life.

At the Thanksgiving Service arranged by Christian Aid when we returned home we were presented with an ancient edition of 'The Pilgrim's Progress'. You remember how it ends – 'And lo, I awoke, and behold it was a dream'.

Thank you for accompanying us, and good luck in your walking.

Journey's End